Vermont Mountain Air for People Stuck Inside

COPYRIGHT © 1999 BY JANE RINCK

All rights reserved under International and Pan-American
copyright conventions
Published in the United States by Al-Jo Press
Any comments or orders:
PO Box 11, Wells Vermont 05774-0011

Illustrations by Jane Rinck
Cover Design by Naomi Rosenblatt
This book was typeset in eleven point Adobe Garamond.
The display face is Adobe Caslon No. 3 italic with swash capitals.
Designed by Mia Novelli
Printed and bound by Inkspot Press, Bennington, Vermont

Library of Congress Cataloguing in Publication Data
ISBN 0-9672969-0-0

To Diana Miller,
my godchild

Contents

. . . And Three Dogs

Introduction

WELCOME TO MY CORNER of Vermont: West Pawlet, a singularly peaceful place. I suspect God takes his Sunday afternoon nap here: perhaps on the hammock slung between two big pine trees in the forest, perhaps in the pasture with the wildflowers and butterflies.

This book is about what it is like to live on the side of a Vermont mountain and vicinity. I came to the mountain fifteen years ago from Ocean County, New Jersey. Three dogs have shared my life here: Josephine a Scotch sheep dog, Al a Welsh Corgi, and Drift a sometime-working sheep dog.

Please do not devour this book in one night. Treat it with the same respect you give to a box of assorted Belgian chocolates: try to make it last, no more than two pieces a day.

My thanks to Marshall Peck of Manchester, Vermont, formerly editor of the Vermont News Guide, who awarded me my first and only literary prize, an antique silver dollar for a letter about George Washington. I have been writing ever since, mostly for the News Guide, occasionally for the Christian Science Monitor. Then along came Ellen Perry Berkeley, editor extraordinaire, better known to me as "Pushy Friend," who never wavered in her belief that my pieces should be in a book, who cheered me onward, who suffered my incredible punctuation and spelling, and who did not give up; a special thanks, PF. Others also cheered and suffered, including Marcia Bravard, Elizabeth Gibson, Maureen Haberer, Jean and Eugene O'Brien, Louise Roby, Judy and Naomi Rosenblatt, and Betty Thomas. And then there is the whole swarm of friends like Roberta Cooper and Bea Griswold, and other News Guide readers who keep asking for more.

Peace to you and enjoy.

Jane Rinck,
West Pawlet

Long Spring

SPRING TAKES HER OWN SWEET TIME in Vermont. She is not for those who require instant gratification. Like a well-made beef stew, she has many ingredients, both subtle and obvious.

She starts early with pale gray banners of maple fog flying from sugar houses all up and down the Mettawee River Valley. The curling sweet mist defies the sullen mountains. That first sip of warm syrup from a Styrofoam cup is true communion with God and His amazing works.

Days or maybe weeks later, Spring flaunts her power with the transformation of ice to water. All the pent-up weight of water, suddenly released, goes tumbling down every mountainside, every ancient gorge, every gentle gradient, seeking the sea. Gravity is not just the fall of an apple, it is a mighty force, well named.

We all have our favorite waterfalls and we ride circuit to revisit them, to stand beside them in fear and delight. I love a certain narrow cascade that flings itself off the top of a mountain in Wells and lands almost on Route 30.

Lambs are part of early spring. To hold a newborn lamb is to hold innocence. To see a sheep with its tiny newborn lamb beside it is to see love and trust. To hear the cry of a lamb looking for its mother is to weep.

Spring is sexy. Oh those spring peepers, ear-splitting racket from invisible thumb-sized beasties—irresistible! And goldfinch, drab all winter, decked out in brightest yellow. Even the owl, notoriously serious, sends his love song across the valley in broad daylight.

Spring has its own colors. Before the apple blossoms come out and leaves unfold, the mountains turn red, changing from their winter gray. In late afternoon when the sun is low, the mountains glow red-purple. Before the grass turns green, we see the deep brown of newly plowed earth, perfect rectangles of rich color. Into this scene, add a chartreuse weeping willow.

Spring is to sit on a rock beside a clump of spring beauties. These tiny pink flowers, about as big as a small fairy, can't be appreciated standing up. I found some beside the mossy roots of an ancient battered maple which was so big around that two friends could not encompass its girth with their arms.

Ferns have not yet sent up their fiddleheads. More is coming. Wait for the lilacs.

Spring Fever

ONE EARLY SPRING DAY when our ancient mountains were swathed in mauve and chartreuse chiffon with occasional dashes of pale gray rain, I just couldn't stay inside. So I took a ride along the river road that follows the Battenkill from Shushan to Arlington. There I saw something that made me stop and back up.

A cream-colored goat was bouncing around on the roof of a substantial doghouse in a barnyard. He had curly fur with matching tail, and small curly horns. His fuzzy ears stuck out from the side and flopped down like big leaves. Now and then he would look down to the ground, obviously amazed to find himself up so high.

Suddenly he leaped to the ground and dashed off in a circle around the barnyard. He stopped briefly for a snack of hay, plunged his head in a nearby wooden bucket for a quick drink of water. Then he went back to his joyful dance on and off the doghouse roof.

I went further along the road going east, upstream, toward Arlington. I saw something else and stopped again. On the other side of the river, high up on a huge dead tree, I saw an unlicensed fisherman with a substantial catch. However, he was not a case for the game warden. The wind ruffled the feathers on his handsome head—an osprey looking like a live Audubon print. He paid no attention to me or to the fancy landscape around him or to the fish; he was concentrating on something upstream. Further up the road I saw the object of his concentration, an unlicensed fisherlady. She also had caught a trout and had a bite or two left under one claw. All at once she was airborne on great brown wings. In a slow, beautiful curve, she glided silently . . . downstream. Spring.

Transition

FOR THOSE WHO LIVE on the south side of a mountain or in sunny valleys, spring, however chilly, has arrived. Not so for those who live on the north side of a mountain or on heights. Here in West Pawlet, spring and winter are playing a giant duet. It is not for us to boast of crocus or of brave snowdrops, those tiny messengers of warmer days. Winter and spring are both here in the same place at the same time, and flowers know better than to become entangled between the two great forces.

The music started weeks ago with a cloud of maple-scented steam from Hulett's sap house floating out over snow-filled fields. We awaken from winter doldrums as from the sound of a trumpet. Change is coming, winter will end. Day by day the white forest floor is transformed into a patchwork quilt of random pattern, brown and white. The brown is the warm of pine needles and old maple leaves, a welcome softness after all winter's stiff, cold white. Around each tree is a circle of brown leaves. All along the brooks, spring has cut brown strips to outline the path of water. Each day the brown grows as the snow retreats.

Meanwhile, the sun has been busy peeling off layers and layers of snow. Off went that top layer, with its ripples like waves. Underneath were the remains of all kinds of animal tracks that still showed their neat stitches across the white quilt. Next uncovered was the sheet of silvery ice that dazzled the eye. Now, all that is left is snow gravel, grainy ice like coarse sand, sprinkled with bits of bark, squirrel-shattered pine cones and fragments of pine needles. A bare handful of this residual snow feels as cold as December and, held up to the sun, sparkles like diamonds.

As ice loosens its grip, spring shatters the silence of winter with water. The mountains sing with it. Never mind the mud, we live with a king's ransom of waterfalls of every possible variety: tall, short, fat, thin, each one with a song of its own.

The huge opera of winter, with its visual fortissimos of swirling clouds, of drifts flung into the air and across roads, its avalanches and tree-cracking cold, slowly lets go. We are almost at the end of winter's long diminuendo. Simultaneously we see and hear the long crescendo of spring. Counterpoint.

Blue Rocks

ONE DAY WHILE my Welsh Corgi Al and I were walking in the forest in an area I do not usually frequent, I came upon a large boulder that was definitely blue. Granite, half buried in the earth, it had obviously been there a long time. Certainly a rock to think about. I memorized its shape and location so I could find it again. Months later, when I was in approximately the same place, I looked for it. I thought I recognized it, but it wasn't blue though it seemed to be the same in size and shape.

Vermont farmers do not share my attitude toward rocks. I like rocks, especially big ones. I came to Vermont from Ocean County in New Jersey, an area once covered by the Atlantic Ocean. When the ocean retreated, it left nothing but sand, no rocks at all. People there who want a rock garden have to buy their rocks, and nicely shaped ones are expensive.

This spring, while clearing away saplings and brush up along the road near the entrance to my driveway, I came upon a very nice rock. A little too small to be called a boulder, it was about twice the size of a basketball, almost round, a pleasant creamy-white color. In New Jersey, it would have been a real winner. I tried to dig it out from its

9

surroundings so I could roll it down the driveway to the garden. I couldn't budge it.

A few days later I went back with a big shovel to try again; no luck, not even a wobble. As I stood contemplating it, I realized it was no longer creamy-white, but blue. Same rock, the very same brilliant blue as the granite boulder in the forest. I crouched down and looked at it up close. The surface was slightly smooth and somewhat translucent: a piece of marble probably brought in by the road department along with other gravel. It had not been painted or moved or touched by anyone since I last saw it. Marble doesn't come that color. I stood up, puzzled, and looked around. I found the answer in the sky.

It was one of those rare spring days when the sky is bluer than blue, an extravagance of color with a depth that goes on and on. Not even one cloud in the way to set a limit. My rock had caught its blue from the sky the same way a pond mirrors what is above it. A perfect match.

I have long known that the forest and all that is in it is bonded to the sky. The great pines reach upward to touch it. The birds seek out the highest branches after cold winter nights to warm themselves in the first rays of the sun. Intrepid tiny spring flowers blossom in those few days before maple leaves come out to cut off their sunlight. Many critters, both large and small, revel in dark sky: moths, fireflies and busy furry bats.

I have long known that the sky has a palette. It paints blue shadows on snow, gold on ice. It spotlights the forest floor through holes in the leafy canopy spread by maple trees. Thus, it picks up a moss-stump here, a white birch there, and it picked out my granite boulder. Incredibly, at sunset, the dark grays of stout trunks are transformed, splashed with brilliant orange. Whole mountainsides are flamed. As the sun sinks, twig by twig the fires blow out, leaving gentle darkness to the shy deer.

But I didn't know about blue rocks. Did you?

River Shopping

WHEN I STARTED OUT for my Sunday afternoon walk with Al, I had no idea that I would come home with all kinds of wonderful presents. The road was clear of snow, ice, and even mud so I decided to walk down the hill to the Mettawee River. The sky was a smooth blue, like the luminous color in medieval Dutch landscape paintings. A day to walk slowly and just look, cows up near the edge of the forest; a touch of red on twigs of distant maple trees to reveal their blossoms, long hidden and still tightly curled up.

On the way, Al stopped off to visit Otto, an elderly lady terrier. (Otto was named before his owner discovered the truth.) I went on alone to the bridge. The river was full and singing with a deep, happy voice, the drought of last summer forgotten. In all of the years of my admiration, I had never seen it so green. Often brown after a storm, often blue reflecting the sky, frequently gray, briefly red when the bottom is covered with autumn leaves, sometimes translucent so I see pebbles and rocks on the bottom. This day it was the color of pine trees.

I left the bridge and went down to the river edge: rocks everywhere. The rocks had all been polished. Three different winter thaws had knocked off all the bits of mud and accumulated algae and scoured them with ice crystals. Late afternoon sun hit them at just the right angle. They glowed and sparkled. Al joined me, cautiously lapping at water's edge. The water was too cold for wading.

Where I came from, stones were rare things. All we had was sand. I was looking at more stones than anyone ever saw in Ocean County. I picked up a hand-sized smooth tan stone. It was a mud sandwich turned into rock layered in different shades of tan of varying thickness, telling a story of ancient floods. It flashed in the sun, a thing of beauty. I pocketed it.

A few steps further along I saw something dark and flat. What was it? I picked it up and found it was wood, a damp thin slab. I turned it over. It was an eagle flying with head thrust forward, legs tucked under, and with a rough surface like feathers. A genuine prize, a gift from the river. I tucked it under my arm.

What else would I find among all the stones? Suddenly I realized that I was standing on a whole shop full of hand-weights. I had meant to buy some for Lisa May's exercise class at the Pawlet Town Hall but hadn't found time to go to a store where they sold such things. I tried several for size and soon found two beauties that fit my hands as if custom carved just for me. Into the pocket.

Before I left I took one more stone to show to a friend for identification: basic gray with a mixture of white chunks and red-brown ovals. I had never seen one quite like it before. I hesitated to take it, not because it was rather big and heavy to carry back up the hill but because it seemed more to belong to the river than the other stones in my pocket. Once I find out about it, I will return it to the river.

But the eagle, I'll keep.

Wolf Tree

SPRING IS A MAGICIAN that plays tricks in my forest. Ferns pretend to be fiddles and boy-frogs plunk pizzicato notes on their bass viols. But the best trick of all is the way certain trees suddenly become bigger. Does the Vermont Institute of Natural Science know about this?

An ancient maple lives up a hill from my house. Foresters would call it a "Wolf Tree" and take it down because it devours light from the young maple progeny that surround it. I suspect that Native Americans ate their lunch under it and the farmer who built the nearby stone wall cooled off in its shade.

The tree is about as shaggy as a tree can ever be. The bark is made up of chunky slabs. Thick branches, some green with lichen, reach far out, defying gravity and also defying any artist who attempts to draw their many convolutions. The tree lost its original top to lightning long ago but sent up a replacement top, slightly off center, now way high up there. Its roots make a comfortable mossy seat. In a hole at the base, some small raisin-eating critter makes a home.

Winter shrinks the tree; it gets smaller. Bare, it clings to its ledge, a gnarled arthritic old man. I worry about it after a storm and trudge up the hill to see how it made out. Sometimes I find that it has dropped a limb or two, but it is a survivor. I go home relieved.

In spring, that tree suddenly becomes huge again. Honest, huge! I have seen it happen for many springs. It just isn't the same size at all. Serene, decked out in pale green with its lavender and gray bark, it tells me "Old can be beautiful."

However, if you come to look at it, bring no tape measure. It has its dignity. Leave it alone or, like any other wolf, it might take a piece out of your ankle.

Vermont Jungle

I DID NOT EXPECT to find jungle in Vermont; by "jungle" I mean a place where trees and vines grow fast, making great tangles requiring a machete to whack your way through, and with lots of insects and wild animals. I thought Vermont was mountains, hay fields, maple syrup and red barns. Wrong. It is jungle.

Vermont jungle has to do with spring and summer. The rest of the year we have that handsome dignified forest that flows over our mountains, down into deep gorges and

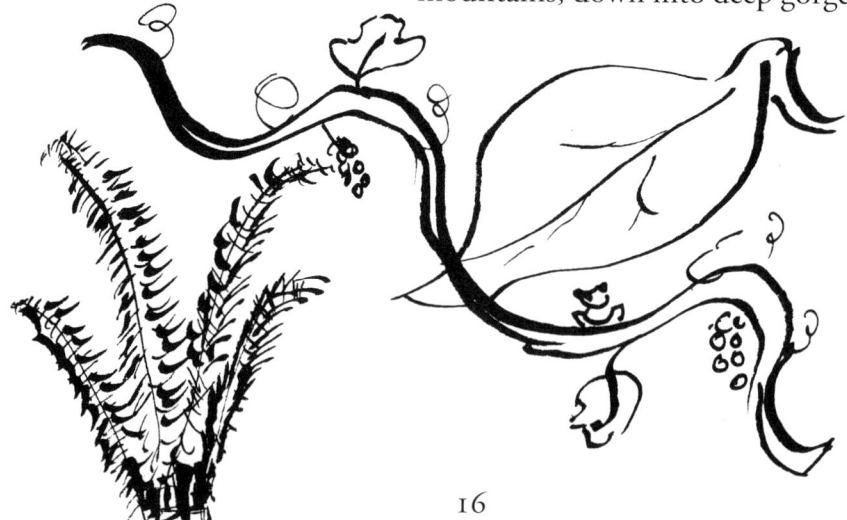

valleys, framing our villages and outlining our rivers. But in spring and summer, nature really cuts loose. Overnight, landmarks disappear behind complex layers of bushes and trees hiding the familiar paths of winter.

Every spring, at the top of my driveway by the mail box, a certain patch of grass defies any reasonable conception of normal grass. Every year I resolve to take a tape-measure with me when I go for the mail to measure its outrageous growth. I always forget. In a very few days that crazy grass is high above my head and swaying in the breeze. I give it no encouragement, no fertilizer, no water, even so it leaps out of soil so abysmally poor and rocky that it took a strong man with a crowbar to dig the post hole for the mailbox.

Grape vines in Vermont are formidable, justly called "wild." The grapes, if you can reach them, are smaller than blueberries and make sharp jelly. Some grape vines have shaggy trunks four or more inches in diameter. Their ropy extensions wrap around trees and climb up to the tops of the tallest pines. They work themselves into massive tangles, stealing light from their tree-victims. Check them out, Tarzan!

Wild cucumber is a fast-acting vine that starts up from a seed each year and is all over the place by August. Its innocent-looking white flowers stand upright like candles, each candle composed of tiny starlets. This charmer sends out long green leafy strings that spin themselves around thorny shoulder-high blackberry and raspberry bushes. Impenetrable.

Jungles tend to be uncomfortable. One of Vermont's jungle meanies is burdock. Burdock is the weed that produces those sticky round balls that have to be cut out of long-haired dogs. Our burdock, left alone, grows into bushes four or more feet high and has leaves as big as the ears of a baby elephant.

The finicky ferns that live in pots inside houses are pathetic compared to the luxuriant ferns of the Vermont forest. In spring our Vermont ferns cover the ground with their fuzzy fiddle heads that unfurl into an intricately patterned ground cover. They come in all sizes; tiny little ones grow in cracks of boulders. Ostrich ferns shoot up tall enough to hide a fair-sized dog, including its tail; such ferns cover areas large enough to throw a mother into a panic should her three-year-old take a notion to wander.

When you walk in a tropical jungle, it comes as a surprise that you don't see many critters, but they are there, well camouflaged. So are ours. While we lack the varieties of a rain forest, our forest is very much alive and especially so in spring and summer. We have a deafening supply of spring peepers, enough mice, moles and voles to feed our owls, moose for amazement, catamounts for mystery, bear for scare and deer for poetry. Each summer we have trees and fields full of visiting tropical birds and butterflies who know a good jungle when they see one. And it all starts from scratch, each spring! Wow!

Fireflies, Anyone?

LATE ONE JUNE NIGHT, I saw a flashlight going past my bedroom window. Somewhat alarmed, I got up and looked out. To my amazement, I beheld a whole constellation of fireflies in the field, blinking their love songs in their special Morse code. I walked out on the deck and watched. Occasionally I looked up at a sky full of more distant stars and wondered what they thought of their earthly competitors.

By August fireflies have almost all vanished. Their silent calls are replaced by love songs of crickets. I wonder what we are doing to these and other small critters of our world. Our huge lawns and power mowers create many local environmental disasters. People with children need running space around their houses Also, dried wildflowers and wild grasses close to a house can be a fire hazard. However, an enormous expanse of lawn is something else: an ego trip, maybe; but surely a repository of strange chemicals, a devourer of time and money, a creator of noise and air pollution, an insult to our natural environment.

As a small gesture to what we foolishly call "civilization," I keep a small twenty-minute lawn and a fifteen-minute garden, complete with tomatoes, parsley, petunias and some rather aggressive Swiss chard. The rest of my land is field and forest.

When I walk down the path through the field, I am surrounded by life. Grasshoppers greet each footstep with Olympic-sized jumps. A large carefully camouflaged toad scrambles away, hoping I don't notice him. Butterflies bounce around, just out of reach. Bees ignore me. A field is as fascinating as a coral reef, and a lot more accessible. Sometimes I go into the field and sit on the ground in the shade of a small cedar tree, disregarding the protest of its resident song-sparrow. At ground level, a field reveals itself. Butterflies seem bigger as they patrol their territory. Emerald beetles walk slowly by. Nothing bites me.

The field is an enormous flower garden, with more flowers than I can count. God ignores the finicky rules of flower arrangers and, for spring, He tosses out great swathes of white daisies and scents the air with assorted pink clovers. He celebrates summer with joyful black-eyed Susans, Queen Anne's lace, and the tall feathers of sweet clover. He finishes the summer with six-foot-tall goldenrod, spicy bergamot and purple asters decorated with monarch butterflies. He flings fluffy milkweed balloons up into blue skies. I neither have to plant nor weed all of this.

We dutifully flatten our tuna-fish cans for recycling and reject the plastic bags at the local supermarket. At the same time we create a botanical wasteland around our homes, a monotonous three-inch carpet that feeds no fireflies, hummingbirds or butterflies. We weep at pictures of oil-soaked sea birds; alas, we are too far away to help them.... But we can save our beautiful countryside with all its magic.

As causes go, this one doesn't fit the usual pattern of earnest effort: meetings, fundraising, brochures, plastic membership cards. It is definitely not for do-gooders. For them, the solution to this environmental nightmare is too easy. But here goes: find an old hammock, tie it between two trees and sleep in it while the grass grows and grows . . . .

Gold Bug

EARLY IN THE MORNING on the last day of June, while sitting on the back step with my second cup of coffee in a not-ready-for-work mood, I gazed in awe at the garden. The lawn was silvery with dew-drops. The long rays of warm sun shone through yellow and blue pansies, making them glow. Birds sang.

A clump of fading pink peonies leaned on the step beside me. My dog Josephine walked by and brushed against it. Petals fell off, making a small heap on green grass. This quiet happening, old dog against old flowers, was a poem, like a gentle death. It was enough to think on, but there was more.

I turned my eyes from the garden to a single complete peony flower, pale pink, right beside me. Her petals were frosted with the tiniest possible dewdrops, each one alight from the sun. She was the ultimate of beautiful. I tried to memorize her:

24

the curves of petals, the deeper pink in the center, the diamond frosting of dew. There was more.

All at once, I noticed a glittering green-gold speck, no bigger than a small crumb, on one pink petal. I wished for my hand lens, but whatever I was looking at might disappear before I could go get it. I took off my glasses and bent down. It was some kind of beetle, slightly tapered at the tail end, wider and blunt at the head with almost invisible corrugations on the body, catching the light. I could just make out two minute antennae and six short legs, all thinner than a hair, alive and moving.

He roamed around on the petal and then, without a qualm, walked along its very edge where it was dry, fearless as a mountain climber walking along the ridge of an alp. He paused and looked down over the edge to the step far below; for me, it would have been like looking down from the top of the World Trade Center. He never noticed me; I was too vast, incomprehensible, like the national debt. Then he wandered off, in and out among the complex petals, a series of soft velvety canyons, a wonderful place to go exploring. At last, he disappeared into the rosy heart of the peony.

I looked down at my knees. They were enormous! I was a giant-giant. Startled, I laughed. I had been looking at the world from the perspective of a mini-beetle.

Giant Emotion, Smallest Bird

ONE SUMMER DAY I had a close encounter with another world, right in West Pawlet. I was practising the violin part of a string quartet in my living room. In spite of my concentration on the music, something made me pause and look out toward the adjacent screened porch. There on the floor I saw what appeared to be a large black butterfly—but the wings were strange. I put down the violin and stepped out on the porch. At my feet was a hummingbird. Its beak had become jammed in the cracks between the boards of the porch floor. It had flown in from the nearby feeder through the open screen door and could not escape, trapped by its long bill.

I reached down. Gently and very easily I pulled the bird free. Immediately it flew up to the screened skylight on the porch ceiling, where it fluttered high out of my reach. I feared that it might get caught in the screen. Suddenly it vanished. I couldn't believe it! Where did it go? I glanced around and quickly discovered it on a low window-sill, motionless, lying on its side. Was it dead?

I stooped down, cupped both hands together and lifted it up. It was weightless, hot, a female with a dark head. Her fairy-size feathers were slightly rumpled, with a touch of white showing. I glanced away; one dares not look at God.

All at once she started to cry—a high clear note repeated over and over. Her cry was of utter despair, giant emotion from a body no bigger than a thimble. Surely emotion has no physical dimension. Her grief went through me. I took her out to the deck and put her down on a large spider plant.

Quicker than my eyes could follow the motion, she was airborne, flying off in a black blur of wings, straight to the forest, back to her nestlings.

I closed the screen door and went back to my violin. Less than a minute had gone by since I'd put it down, but I could not bring myself to pick it up. I had held a live, hot crown jewel in these, my hands. I walked around the room. When I finally returned to my music, the notes seemed very large and the sounds crude. Beethoven's complex eloquence was no match for the sound that came from the smallest bird of God.

The Escape of a Red Eft

WHILE WALKING in the forest, after a rainstorm had finally ended a long drought, I came upon a group of red efts. They had come out from under rocks where they had been sheltering during the drought. I reached down and picked one up to have a look.

A red eft is a newt. A newt is a lot like a salamander, but has a fancy life style. It starts out life swimming around in a pond dressed in drab greenish brown. After a year of this, it crawls out of the pond, turns a spectacular shade of orange-red and lives on the forest floor. Red efts don't bite. They are not slimy. Children can pick them up without being afraid.

The smallness of it is what started me thinking. If the red eft in my hand had encountered that famous elf who invented the umbrella by snatching up a toadstool to keep off the rain, my eft would scarcely have come up to the top of

28

the elf's pointy green shoes. Yet, in spite of its small size, my eft was well equipped. Its four legs, a bit bow-legged, operated the same way as an alligator's. It had a lizard-shaped snout and bright eyes. I wanted to see if its eyes were the same as turtle eyes, but it wouldn't hold still. No way.

That small creature wanted to get away. It kept crawling across my palm to the edge. I shifted it to my other hand, and it crawled to the edge of that hand and so on, from hand to hand. I meant it no harm, didn't want it to fall, a distance in people-proportions comparable to a leap from the top of the Grand Canyon. In spite of my efforts, that determined critter managed to slip through my fingers and fall to the ground. I saw it crawl away and disappear under a fragment of a leaf. Gravity doesn't get serious about such tiny objects, no heavier than the tail-feather of a blue jay.

That eft knew what it wanted. It wanted to escape, and it kept at it until it succeeded. I have found that frogs, toads, and grasshoppers always manage to slip through my fingers. Butterflies are not speedy, and yet they are often clever enough to dodge a net. Trout shake off a hook, and birds fly high out of reach when you get too close. Bears vanish when they hear a hiker who ties bells on his shoelaces. Field and forest are full of animals both great and small that run from us if they hear, see or smell us coming. They also hide from each other to avoid becoming lunch. Only after the snow is on the ground can we see the elaborate network of tracks that reveals their secretive comings and goings.

People have the same built-in urge to escape as do the red eft and all the rest of nature's critters. A two-month-old baby I recently attempted to hold turned bright red from head to toe, stiffened up her entire body, and let out ear shattering sounds. I soon gave her back to her mom. Toddlers can escape in a blink. Adults have made glorious escapes, starting with all our forefathers and continuing with many others, including flatlanders from New Jersey who now inhabit Vermont.

The urge to escape is a force more powerful than hunger, next only to the need for air and water. It has to do with who we are and who we would be. It is the root of freedom, an innate force that we share with other living creatures. The forest teaches humility. When I picked up that wee red eft, I did not appreciate the fact that we had anything in common. Just the same, I wish that the wonderful creatures of the forest would not run from me, for I mean them no harm. But how can they know? Alas, we suffer from a failure of communication. We just don't speak the same language.

Cow Pasture

MY NEIGHBOR Eunice Hill calls my place in West Pawlet "The Cow Pasture." Many years ago, she used to walk up the hill to the pasture to bring her cows down to Ed Hill's barn to be milked, a distance of about a quarter of a mile. The pasture must have looked quite different then with the cows keeping grasses eaten up. Now, under my jurisdiction, the pasture is shaggy. Vermont farmers would not approve.

Unattended, the pasture rapidly reverts to forest. Every two or three years, I have someone cut back its excesses with a brush-hog machine. The window of opportunity for brush-hogging is brief, after the snow melts but before the thaw turns the land to mud that would swallow the machine, and also before the birds make their nests. Matt Solon, a Pawlet artist, offered to do the not-so-easy job. He emerged by four o'clock, bleeding from the savage thorns of ten-foot-long strands of blackberry bushes.

For a short time the pasture was bare except for dried-up and flattened remains of old brush. Soon a thin veil of green found its way through. Then came the El Niño rain. Plants took off, exploded into growth in volume and height I had not seen in my fifteen years of living at the pasture.

Goldenrod grew from its usual two to four feet height to five to ten feet and appeared in places where it had never been before. It blocked up pathways through the field and overwhelmed blackberries. Bergamot, that spicy lavender beauty, doubled in height. Vetch made a foot-deep spongy rug of pink flowers and wrapped its delicate tendrils around giant-sized milkweed. Jerusalem artichokes challenged the flag pole. Wild cucumber vines strung green ropes with white candles all the way to the top of a young aspen, decorating it like a Christmas tree. Queen Anne's lace established a significant statement by the drive-way where previously only two or three once gathered. Even meadow-sweet, usually of modest demeanor, reached up.

To stand in the pasture this summer is almost frightening. It is as if I had suddenly become a foot shorter, a child who has to look up and who can't see over the tops of things. I stand surrounded by familiar flower-friends who have suddenly become bigger and taller. Instead of looking down at flowers, I have a butterfly's view of blossoms and an intimate view of bees at work. Up close, it is obvious that each goldenrod flower is really a composite of approximately one hundred or more tiny flowers. A pasture full of such flowerlets may well be the equivalent of all the stars of our solar system, and just the right color.

To say the pasture is lovely is understatement. When the long rays of the late afternoon sun light up the goldenrod from the side, for a few brief moments, the whole pasture is alight with gold fire: a splendor.

All this emerged from bare earth, tiny seeds, a thin layer of rock-infested soil, and that rain: a live miracle. "El Niño" is Spanish for "The Baby Jesus."

Breakfast with a Flower

A FRIEND WHO WAS MOVING to smaller quarters phoned me one day to ask if I wanted her night-blooming Cereus plant. Not knowing exactly what I was getting, I said, "yes." It turned out to be a cactus, a four-foot-tall, slim, gray-green column with thorny ridges in a large heavy pot. We rolled it up in newspapers and gingerly laid it in the back of my station wagon. Now it inhabits a plant bench in my living room in windows facing south. Because it leans slightly to starboard, I placed some heavy rocks on one side of the pot as a counterweight.

I have had it several years now and know its ways. Its flowering is an event, for it only blooms once a year, and maybe not even that. It blooms only at night, for only one night with one flower. At dawn, the flower dies.

This summer, I noticed a green bump about the size of a child's thumb protruding near the top of the column on the edge of one of the thorny ridges. I knew that the plant was going to give birth. Every day I checked its progress. In three days the bump changed into a three-inch oval bud with pale green spiraling petals hiding the white flower inside. The bud was fastened to the column by a long green stem. By the fourth day, I could see the edges of the inner white flower still wrapped in pale green outer petals. The stem, now almost as thick as a thimble, poked out several inches from the column, thus holding the bud well away from thorns. The speed with which the bright green stem and intricate bud emerge from the drab column is startling.

On that fourth night, I had a ticket to a concert in Manchester. I was concerned that the flower might come and go in my absence, so I left home with reluctance. When I returned, my head was full of Beethoven, and I forgot to look at the plant. The next morning it was still dark when I awoke but night was over, and dawn about to step on stage. I remembered the flower. Was I too late? I hastened to look.

Yes, the bud had opened. The flower was still in its night-time glory. Twenty or more overlapping tapered white petals stretched out, cup-shaped, and large as a man's hand; in the center, an inner circle of delicate white stamens, yellow tipped; the back of the flower supported by the pale green petals now in the shape of a star. All this, at the top of the column with its thorns.

Even though I have seen this event before, each time it happens the flower seems to call to me as if it wants to say something important. You can't turn your back on such a flower. I brought my breakfast on a tray and sat beside it, as one does with a beloved.

We sat in silence together, the flower and I. The shortness of its life intensified the beauty and significance of its life the same way as it did for Jesus: a death watch, but curiously peaceable.

Darkness melted into pink dawn, then into daylight. As imperceptibly as the motion of a sailboat, in a gentle breeze so light that the boat seems becalmed yet still moves across a horizon, so the white

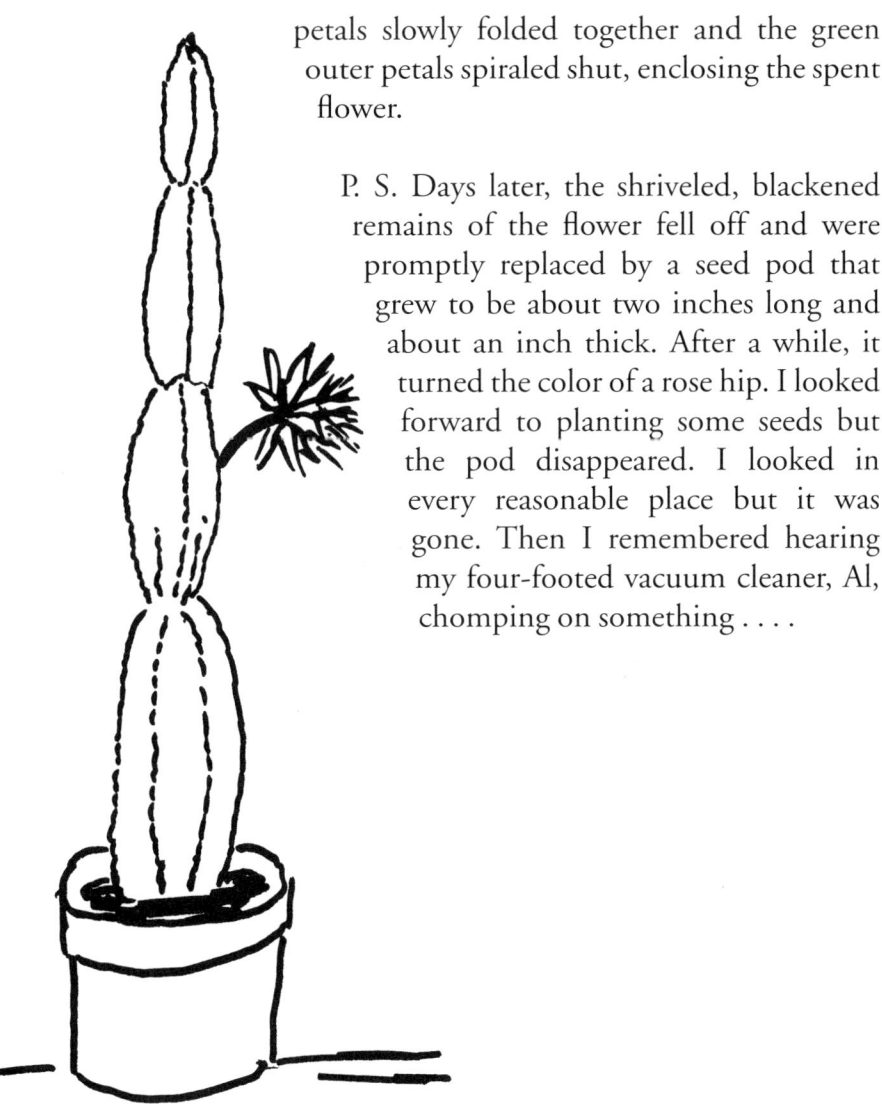

petals slowly folded together and the green outer petals spiraled shut, enclosing the spent flower.

P. S. Days later, the shriveled, blackened remains of the flower fell off and were promptly replaced by a seed pod that grew to be about two inches long and about an inch thick. After a while, it turned the color of a rose hip. I looked forward to planting some seeds but the pod disappeared. I looked in every reasonable place but it was gone. Then I remembered hearing my four-footed vacuum cleaner, Al, chomping on something . . . .

The Railroad Track Secret

VERMONT IS FULL OF GREAT but secret places. Well, not exactly secret, but places so casually mentioned that you don't pay attention. You can live in a town for years and, even when driving slowly, you can go right past waterfalls, ponds, or deep, cool swimming holes, almost but not quite in plain sight. They are known by all children, but not by all adults, certainly not by flatlanders from New Jersey.

One summer I bought a mountain bike. After trying to bike up my steep driveway to the mailbox, I quickly discovered that I was no mountaineer. I was saved from disgrace by the Rail-Trail, one of those secret places. Children told me how to find it. Vermont has miles of abandoned railroad tracks that have been stripped of rails and ties and surfaced with fine gravel. They are called "Rail-Trails."

I get on the Trail near Dutchy's store in West Pawlet. I bike early in the morning while the mist hangs low in the cornfields, before the sun is hot. I walk my bike across the modified remains of the old railroad bridge over the Indian River so I can enjoy its bright water. Then I follow the Trail through cool forest. I pass two small factories, both still working, and wave at the people inside. They wave back. The valley opens up.

Who would expect to find poetry on a railroad track? Yet, there it is, spread out all over the valley. The scene before me resembles French countryside as I have seen it in the landscape paintings of Corot. A straight path extends for miles and dissolves in the distance into a pale blue circle of light. Above is the vast arch of sky, uninterrupted by mountains and hung each day with different clouds: cirrus, alto stratus, cumulus, and an occasional cumulo nimbus with rays of light streaking out. Sky is important!

The very straightness of the path is curiously relaxing. Vermont roads are as full of curves as a bowl of spaghetti. The almost level ground is also rare; most of Vermont is either up or down. Trail biking is easy, unlike so many difficult things of which life is full. My biking style in no way resembles that of serious racers who fly by on the edge of highways, crouched over looking at the pavement. The Trail deserves to be savored at a slow pace. I stop at a certain small bridge and lean on its railing to check out a small brook, I get off to examine a tree full of birds, I pause to admire a deer.

Cornfields are everywhere. They have a special majesty as they grow from bare earth, to tender shoots, to glorious tasseled height, then pale tan death. Each day changes the procession of wild flowers, from the white stars of blood root in early spring, on to blue chickory, purple bergamot with its spicy smell, and finally goldenrod. All these and more line the side of the path. Rabbits freeze on the pathway, hoping not to be noticed, then dash off into the raspberry bushes to hide. The great blue heron sees me coming and takes off. Certain birds fly right along with me, keeping two bushes ahead. Bird watching at its very best.

Here's to the Rail-Trail! Chug Chug Toot Toot!

Bike-Seeing

WHEN SIGHT-SEEING, you go to some predetermined place to look at something with a known reputation for being educational, unique, beautiful. When bike-seeing, you discover things that were there all along but missed because you have been whizzing by them in a car. The bike makes this possible because it enhances our natural power of locomotion, and like a canoe, extends our range without wearying our feet. Bike-seeing is fun; sight-seeing can be heavy.

To ride around your own neighborhood on a bike can be a joy. My neighborhood is West Pawlet. We have some lovely gardens in plain sight, but with charming details invisible at thirty miles or more per hour. One is a perfect Dutch garden complete with a mini-waterfall and neatly spaced petunias worthy of the Boston flower show. Another is a side-yard garden with glorious peonies, poppies, lots of delphiniums, and amazing lilies. Many houses have window-box gardens and, on porches, luxuriantly blooming hanging baskets. The Post Office is a delight. West Pawlet loves flowers.

At bike-pace, you can see into back yards with vegetable gardens of deep brown soil where plants grow in precise rows like West Pointers on parade. Vermonters are serious about vegetable gardens. No weeds allowed!

Backyards tell a human story. Clotheslines reveal not only the age and number of inhabitants in the house, but also the good character of the homemaker who understands the luxury of the scent of sun-dried sheets. Rope-swings hang from trees waiting for children. Clusters of lawn chairs stand ready for gatherings of friends and family, and barbecues. People in such houses know how to live.

Those padded motorized metal boxes we ride around in cut us off from smells, one of our most fundamental senses. On a bike we breathe in the heartwarming smells of summer: clover, cool forest, freshly mowed hay, hamburgers cooking. One day as I was pedaling along, I came upon a lovely clump of perfumed air. I stopped, got off to look for its source. Nothing at ground level. I looked up. High up at the crown of a row of ancient locust trees was a mass of creamy white blossoms. Ah . . . .

Bikes have no windshields. You are out in the air with all kinds of critters. You get to know where they live. A wood-thrush sings in a certain patch of forest; a red-tailed hawk watches for a mouse from a certain tree. A certain large dog bounds out from a farm and makes a

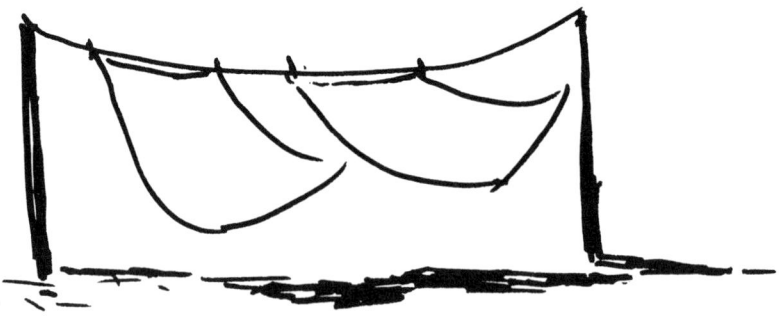

loud "woof woof" and retreats, smugly muttering to himself, "Well, by golly, I sure scared her away."

You rediscover wind on a bike and, like sailors, you always know its direction. Down wind gives you a free ride, up wind turns flat places into hills. Wind blowing through a cornfield is like wind over water, blowing long green satin leaves into waves. As you go flying down hills on a bike you feel the rush of air on your face, through your hair, and over your whole body.

On a bike, you rediscover shadows. You feel the sudden cool and dark as you go into a forest with its floor of fern. Moments later, you burst out into brilliant heat and sun, a field blanketed with thousands of dandelions, two entirely different worlds of plants, animals and insects: field and forest, back to back.

Sight-seeing is often a mob scene, the more famous the sight, the bigger the mob. The little mermaid who gazes out from her rock in Copenhagen harbor has long lost her privacy to tour bus-loads. Bike-seeing can be solitary, peaceful; no phone to ring, no dishwasher to gurgle, no TV to chatter away. By bike, sounds are simple, an occasional click as you change gears, bird songs, a friendly "Good morning" called out by a stranger. No one knows where you are. You have disappeared, gone biking: call it "freedom."

Corn

AS SUMMER ADVANCES, corn becomes massive in Vermont. Ten-foot-high green walls line our roads, hiding all but high mountains behind them. The walls enclose an almost solid mass of vegetation many square acres in size. This world of interlocking stalks and leaves responds to wind with ripples and waves like the waters of a lake. It is a hiding place for deer and thieving raccoons. Absolutely beyond belief, it will all eventually be converted into cheddar cheese, yogurt and milk!

The curious thing about these magnificent walls and the worlds behind them is that no one ever talks about them, with the exception of farmers who live in a special world of their own. They are expert worriers; corn is their life. The rest of the population goes by at fifty or more miles per hour without comment.

Imagine if ten square acres of something else were to gradually accumulate along Route 30, consider the outcry: ten square acres of used cars, of stones, of boxes of cereal, of apartments, of ice cream? No one complains about the corn. It is benign. But how can it be so taken for granted?

A corn seed is no bigger than a thumbnail. Yet it grows into a plant ten feet tall. Rippled leaves shed rain. Neatly packaged fruit of gold or white satin swells, the result of a beautiful reproductive system made in part with silken thread. And, Oh, the taste of it, fresh out of a field . . . . *Then* everyone notices the corn.

Cows and corn are one of nature's partnerships. Add to it, the farmer who clears the field, tends the soil and plants the seed. Rain does her part. The result is a miracle. Just because it happens millions of times each year beginning from each small seed doesn't diminish the wonder of it all.

We look at the bare fields all winter, sometimes gleaming with ice, sometimes sparkling with snow. We see the freshly turned dark earth in spring, followed by the precise rows of tiny shoots, and are gladdened. We watch the steady growth of stalks as they reach upward. After a while, the rows slowly disappear as the leaves reach across the rows to touch their neighbors.

When the corn reaches its full height, "high as an elephant's eye" in Vermont as in Oklahoma, trumpets should sound at this recurring miracle, as we sound them for Christmas.

In spite of all the sorrows of the past year, of conflicts and disasters, of storms and crashes, of deaths and disappointments, the earth still works. The seed, the soil, the cows, the man, the rain; God's system endures.

Horse Close-Up

I HAVE A FRIEND, Penny, who likes to explore back roads and is fearless about talking to strangers. Consequently she finds some really nifty places. One day she took me to a place that has a herd of Lipizzaner horses. Lipizzaners in Danby? In Vermont anything is possible.

Lipizzaners are those horses especially cherished in Vienna. The Viennese train them to waltz the "Blue Danube" in a splendid marble horse palace. The trainer at the farm told us that Julius Caesar brought Lipizzaners from Arabia for his army. Their extra large size was useful for trampling the enemy. Colts are born black, gradually turn gray-brown and finally purest white.

I enjoy sketching animals and I have a friend Judy who likes to photograph them. One Sunday afternoon, we set out to do the horses. Sun shone on our expedition. We were cordially greeted by staff, shown the access gates to the fields, and warned about electric fences. They also told us that it might be hard to draw and photograph because the horses would get in the way. I didn't think this would be a problem, but I didn't know much about horses. I'd had riding lessons in the third grade, but since then I'd admired horses from a discreet distance.

After spotting a herd on a distant hill, we passed through the first gate, reclosed it and crossed a field toward the herd. A large gray-brown horse came walking over and stopped right up close to me, head to head. Though he was big and startling (I am used to a Welsh Corgi only inches high), he was not hostile. He had come to greet me the way my doggie comes up to visitors, welcoming. I reached up and rubbed his nose. Then he plunged it into my jacket pocket, sniffing vigorously. Sorry, no carrots.

We unwrapped the chain at the second gate and slid quickly through to the field with the herd. By the time we had secured the gate, six or seven young gray-brown horses had arrived to greet us. What a greeting! In moments I was surrounded by a circle of huge horse heads. Being short, I could only see heads: long noses to be patted, wiggly ears, eyes with long lashes, shaggy hair hanging down fore-heads. They pushed and shoved to get as close as possible to us, like a bunch of kids wanting lollipops.

Horses do have a whole lot of nose. It startled me to see a horse nostril three or four inches from my eyes. A horse nostril is very large and deep, shaped like a giant comma. I saw that horses have thick rub-bery lips and lots of whiskers. They were interested in my sketch pad and attempted to sample it with their surprisingly sensitive and gentle lips. The metal clip that holds paper to my drawing board got knocked off. An extra large, sandpaper-warm tongue licked my arm. Even Rembrandt would have had trouble drawing under such conditions. I wasted a lot of paper, but Judy got some great pictures.

Horse ears are strong and important looking, lily shaped, dark and fuzzy inside and securely fastened to a base that you don't notice from a distance. I kept smelling something nice. It wasn't a wet dog smell, not manure, not cow, not sweet like a flower, though I looked around to see if something was in bloom nearby. That clean woody smell, a cross between a mushroom and an apple blossom, was horse!

Suddenly I knew where I had seen horses like these before: The British Museum, carved out of white marble, huge and handsome, once on the Parthenon and now in Danby. I was standing right in the middle of a live Greek frieze.

The only white horse in the field was Belinda, a retiree, sway-backed. She was considerably larger than the younger gray-brown horses. She demanded my attention, bumping me and shoving the others away. Not a horse to ignore, insistent. What was she trying to say?

Just as some very old women are still beautiful, perhaps because of their spirit, so the old horse was still beautiful When she held her great white head on its still powerful neck with white mane against blue Vermont sky, well, call it poetry.

Trail Flowers

ONE MORNING in early August, I went biking on the West Pawlet part of the Rail-Trail. I pedaled through the forest, over the two bridges, past the two factories, one leaking music and the other thumping, and then I was in the Indian River Valley. A blue sky day. I hadn't been biking since April. I was not prepared for what I saw.

On each side of the Trail, as far as eye could see, stretched a double border of fluffy lavender flowers floating in clouds of their pale gray-green foliage: tiny leaves, thousands of flowers, flowers by the mile. I got off the bike and just looked. Awesome, like seeing a double rainbow or suddenly confronting the ocean beyond a big sand dune.

As I stood there, I could almost hear a soft but insistent voice coming from a flower saying, "Where have you been? Where have you been? You missed the daisies. You haven't been here since the bloodroot was in bloom." I thought about making some excuses but somehow I had the distinct impression that they would not be accepted. As I continued along on my bike, the flower's question circled in my mind. "Where have you been?"

Interspersed among the lavender flowers were many old friends: sunny St. Johnswort, heavenly blue chicory, fat pink clover, handsome Joe Pye weed, virgin's bower vine, all white and lacy like brides' trains, and more. I looked up the lavender border flower in Peterson's when I got home: Tyrol knot-weed.

The Trail flowers all looked so prosperous and comfortable. Their many colors seemed deliberately arranged to complement one another. Similarly, their various heights were arranged with short flowers in front and tall ones in back. The flowers accomplished this without the help of a landscape designer. Their healthy condition was not assisted by a gardener with dirty broken fingernails, five-ten-five plant food or bags of mulch. None of the flowers came out of little plastic boxes, six small plants for $2.98.

If a weed is a plant in the wrong place then what I was seeing were not weeds at all. They were just where they belonged, obviously flourishing. No one had to weed them. Like birds in the spring, each had established its own territory to raise the next generation.

Was I looking at second-rate flowers? Not at all. Bergamot with its shaggy purple petals is listed as a wildflower but finds its way into tame gardens, where it takes on other colors. For sheer beauty, consider Queen Anne's lace, a great flower, well named. In France, goldenrod grows wild but is an honored garden flower. On the Trail, goldenrod was everywhere, bowing gently swaying in the breeze. Ah, the Canada lilies, so beautiful and shy, meriting a blue ribbon. Every year a wildflower sneaks into my tame garden: buttercups, daisies, Queen Anne's lace. I let them stay.

The narrow path of the Trail is mowed by volunteers. The wide border is left to grow wild. Spikes of unpunished grass, silver beige—tall as my bike wheel, thin as an etcher's line—nodded in clumps beside the path. The delicate design of the seed tassels reminded me of something special: Ah, that's it, a crystal chandelier. Artists are always getting their best designs from nature.

As I look beyond the Trail to certain uncultivated fields, wildflowers make huge splashes of color, the color of dawn or sunset come to earth. Color the way our primitive ancestors saw it. Glorious.

All the way home I kept hearing that soft voice saying, "Where have you been? Where have you been?" And where have we all been? We need to consider the lilies of the field.

Dog Walk

ONE WARM DAY in late August I was peacefully reading in a hammock under pine trees when my dog Josephine nudged me. "Want to go for a walk?" she asked, drilling me with her deep brown eyes half hidden under long shaggy white hair. "Well, all right, if you insist," I replied.

Usually when we went for walks, I was the one who decided where to go and led the way. Then, when I was ready to go home, I followed her because she always knew the shortest route. This time I would see where Josephine would take me.

She bounded off through the field. Purple and gold swirled around us in huge clumps of wild bergamot and shoulder-high goldenrod. Added to these were white clouds of sweet clover, a dash of orange black-eyed Susans, and pink meadowsweet. Three yellow butterflies twirled above us. I paused to admire my carefree garden, but Josey glanced back at me and asked, "Well, are you coming?"

I followed her on through a patch of young aspens, then across a ditch and on into my neighbor's cornfield. Up close, corn is impressive. Each stout stalk is firmly rooted, drawing its strength from the earth. The color "green" surrounded me in all its rich variety from the palest yellow to the deepest emerald. Corn towered high over my head, obliterating the blue sky. Small explosions of tawny silk decorated the tightly wrapped ears. As I walked along between the first two rows of the huge field, long tapered leaves, rough on top and satin smooth beneath, brushed against my face.

We left the field and followed a deer trail into the forest. Josey knows all of them in our territory. Some are deep-cut by generations of deer who have passed along them, silently. In thick brush, they disappear to the eye but you can feel them underfoot. Josey finds them by nose.

We headed for the river and came to the flood plain forest, cool and still: a magical place. Acres of ostrich fern completely hid the earth, the deer trail and all of the dog except the tip of her tail. Huge sycamore trees dimmed the light.

We arrived at the Mettawee River. Josey walked in and lapped. I settled down on a big boulder, took off my boots and socks and dabbled my feet in the clear cool water. The bottom of the river is covered with all kinds of stones. I picked up some to admire their colors and to check out the small critters living on their undersides. Josey walked out into the middle where the swifter current and deeper water fluttered through her long fur. Finally she came over to my boulder, licked one of my feet by way of comment, then snuggled up next to me, all damp.

We sat there looking at the shimmering river. "Josephine," I said, "things don't get any better than this."

Harvest Time

SOME DAYS ARE JUST too beautiful to waste on duty. September 26, 1998, in particular, was such a day. It began with mist that blotted out the whole landscape, except for the doves eating sunflower seeds on my deck railing. Doves in mist: a Japanese poem waiting for an artist with bamboo-handled brush and rice paper. When the sun came out from behind the mountain, it chased away the mist and lighted up a cloudless sky. Air was like water from a cold spring. The only thing to do on such a day is to stay outside: leave behind the clutter of household and mind.

Al and I took off down the road at a fast clip, Al leading the way but looking back frequently to be certain he was leading in the right direction. About a mile down the road, I noticed that a gate usually barring access to a private road was open. This was the day to go down that road, something I had long wanted to do.

We were on an old road with stone walls on both sides, the labor of long-departed men with calloused hands and strong backs. The branches of tall trees met across the road, making it a shady arched green tunnel. Al splashed through puddles in deep ruts, taking an occasional lap of rainwater left over from the previous night. Muddy horseshoe tracks in the center of the road told of an unknown early morning rider. Curves in the road, as it wound around the mountain, led me on and on.

Then I noticed the hickory nuts right at my feet. They fall to earth in an oval, bright green package cleverly designed so that they

split apart on impact. The delicious nut inside is pale cream color and requires a very determined person or squirrel to extract it. Soon I had two pocketsful and wished I had brought a bag.

We had been going uphill. We came to a field and made a brief side trip to inspect it. Who had cleared this isolated field? No farmhouse was in sight for miles around. As we stood in the sunshine, a bird, possibly a flicker, came out of the trees and sat on a bush and complained loudly at our presence in his domain.

Further on, we came to a hunting camp, soon to be full of eager men. A high bar fastened between two trees would hold several dead deer. Masculine territory. We went on.

We came to an open space, clear of brush, flooded with sunshine, a place of thin soil, rock, moss, and wiry grass that has the look of a lawn. A scattering of pines and birches made it seem like a park, a place for a picnic. I sat down on soft moss and rested in the sunshine and blue sky while Al, tireless, explored with all the power of his super-sensitive nose, big ears, and brown eyes.

On the way back, I saw a group of small puffballs fastened to a rotting log. Puffballs are mushrooms, easy to identify, delicious sautéed in butter. I added them to the hickory nuts in my pocket. Back on my own road, as I was passing my neighbor's house, I heard a call. It was Dave Clark with two pears in his hand from his organic orchard. How could I be so lucky? Great neighbor, great pears. By the time I got home I had eaten them both.

That afternoon I went on my bike to West Pawlet along the Rail-Trail. Fields were bare of corn, and I saw a large flock of crows circle over them and disappear beyond a distant hill. A blue heron lifted up from the stream when it saw me coming.

A snow-white puffball, big as a man's hand, brought me to a halt. I fastened it to the rack on the back of my bike. Fallen butternuts stopped me next; again I wished for a bag because they are sticky. Black walnuts that I came upon were almost more than I could handle. They are big and round. I had a hard time stuffing them into my pockets; they kept falling out and rolling away. I made one last stop to taste the remains of wild raspberries that grow all along the edge of the Trail. I went home laughing; I was a chipmunk with bulging pockets.

At sundown, a friend Sharon stopped by with her four-year-old son, Andy. To my amazement, my incredible harvest continued. She had brought me a squash, cheese, refried beans and more laughter.

Much later, I put on a warm coat and took a chair up to the road where there is a good view of the eastern sky. From there I could see the last full-moon eclipse of the century. I waited in the silent cold. Brilliant moonlight slowly melted into starlight as the shadow of earth moved over the ancient face of the moon, turning it pink. Finally, it hung high above the dark mountain up among the stars, a great round Japanese lantern. A day to remember.

Pondie

VERMONT FORESTS are full of secrets. Because the terrain is so irregular—full of gorges, shaggy cliffs, steep hills and deep valleys—it is not always possible to see far ahead. Also, the foliage, especially in summer, is thick: brush, small trees, big fallen trees complete with huge branches, and great tangles of roots. Not only is it easy to get lost, it is also possible to miss something delightful. Wonderful for exploring.

One Sunday in early autumn, Al and I climbed over the old broken-down stone wall of my north boundary, a place I had not explored because it is squishy and gloomy. Rusty remains of a barbed wire fence on the other side of the wall threatened my ankles. We were in a mini-valley, its steep hills enclosing a swampy bottom. Soon we came to a series of long lateral rock outcroppings shaped like the tops of half-buried dinosaurs, gray, sharp, unfriendly. We had to climb over each one. On top of the highest one we paused to look around. Because he is so short, Al never misses a chance to get up high. Off to the right in the swampy area, the gray branches of a group of small dead trees poked upwards. Perhaps water from a beaver dam had killed them? We climbed down to take a closer look. Sure enough, the dead branches were standing in bright blue water, along with a great blue heron that unfolded its wings and flew off, disturbed by our intrusion. We had come to a pond. We followed the edge, Al smiling as he sent frightened frogs into deeper water. The underbrush thinned out, and we could see a long stretch of water. The shoreline was steep rock covered with moss and brown pine needles. We came to a low rocky peninsula, and I plopped down on soft moss.

Bright blue water covered an area about the size and shape of a football field. Gentle puffs of wind ruffled the surface and pushed along a few yellow fallen leaves: miniature sailboats. Cortez or Balboa standing on that peak looking out at the Pacific could not have been happier than I. Discovery is a rarely experienced delight.

On the far shore, a steep forested bank with red and gold maples was doubled upside down by reflection in the shining water. Not a sound, except for an occasional splash of frog dislodged by Al scouting along the edge. No evidence of humanity, not even one beer can. Clear water, a place to swim and picnic, less than a half hour's hike from my house, has been there all this time . . . .

Just off the far shore, I saw a ripple. Was it a fish? I kept looking. Something was sticking up . . . turtle perhaps? Yes, it was a turtle, and it was coming toward us, not fast but not slow either. In water, turtles can easily beat even a dutiful rabbit. The closer it came, the bigger it got, and still bigger. MIGHTY BIG and coming straight at us. The top of its pointy shell poked up out of the water quite far from the place where the long neck and head stuck up.

The wrinkled neck was mottled, brownish with a nasty red streak. Its reptile head was as big as my fist, and its beak could snap off a thumb. At fifteen feet I could see that it was looking me right in the eye with a large blurry stare. Why is it OK for me to look at a turtle but unsettling for a turtle to look at me? It had my complete attention, except . . . .

Maybe it happened when I glanced away to see if Al was out of reach, or maybe it was when I blinked. The turtle vanished. Gone, silently, and without leaving so much as a ripple or even a bubble. Nothing.

Al and I have been back to the pond many times since, not to swim or picnic but to look for that turtle. Never there. Like Champie and Nessie, genuine dragons are shy.

I have often wondered why the old turtle crossed the pond. Was it hungry, hoping for a good last meal before the pond froze for the winter? Was it asserting its proprietary rights saying, "MY POND"? Was it bored, lonely or just curious? What do turtles think about?

Of one thing I am sure: never miss a chance to step over an ancient barrier. You never quite know what is on the other side. It can sometimes be great.

Tree Sculpture

MY LAND IS SHAPED like a long rectangle bounded by a tumbled down stone wall and bits of rusty barbed wire. Beyond it is a similar tract quite different in character. I call it the "magic forest." It has very little underbrush, a steep hill, a rocky cliff and a carpet of beautiful wild grass: great place for a Sunday afternoon walk with my dog. In fifteen years, I have never encountered anyone else there. Now and then the deer and I startle each other. It is a very private place.

About five years ago, I there made a discovery. At the top of the hill I came upon the trunk of an ancient broken dead maple, and beyond it another, and beyond that, still more. I was in an art gallery of two-hundred-year-old fallen giants with ten-foot-tall trunks still clinging to earth by gnarled roots and surrounded with thick, twisted, fallen branches. The colors of their shaggy bark are too subtle to name: colors that change as sunlight moves around huge trunks.

This is no ordinary art gallery, not a place to rush through, where mind and feet become numb; but rather a place with plenty of moss-covered seats where you can sit, eat a peanut butter sandwich, give your dog a drink of water, and take your time.

You are in an outdoor sculpture gallery. Each tree has a unique shape. Sculptors love the shape of things. Not for them the flatness of

two-dimensional TV or computer screens, they prefer all three juicy dimensions. Sculpture feeds the soul.

One of the tests of great sculpture is that nothing will break off if you roll it down a steep hill. The old trees meet this test. You see powerful trunks, scarred by lightning, shattered where huge branches tore off in wind, twisted by snows and gales, hollowed by decay, fingers pointing up, remains of branches reaching out.

These indomitable old fellows are a presence. A funny presence. One tree has a three-foot-long beak, a knothole eye and splinter feathers that stick straight up on the top of its head. Another is being attacked by a long snaky dragonbranch. If you walk around another tree and stop at just the right place, you can make out a wonderful eagle taking off at full speed. At the base of one, a smiling alligator is swallowing a big branch. Several have great big holes that become scary eyes, and mouths that howl silently.

Guess where you can find similar dragons, huge flying birds, strange faces, and all kinds of critters doing extraordinary things . . . . Find a place where there is a good view of the sky, preferably on a sunny day with lots of wind. Then look up. There you may see a fluffy white bird chasing a camel who is following grandma smoking a pipe!

Cloud-watching is not just for kids!

Autumn Cathedral

IN THE HEART of Paris is an island in the Seine River. In the middle of the island is a large palace, Le Palais de Justice, and in the middle of the palace is an ancient chapel, La Sainte Chapelle. You enter it from an insignificant, short staircase off in a corner. At the top, you step out into an immense jewel; you are inside a ruby-sapphire-emerald. Walls made of tiny pieces of brilliantly colored stained glass reach from floor to sky, filling the air with living color. When the sun shines through the glass . . . *magnifique*!

For a few days in October, on a hillside in Pawlet, far from Paris, the spiritual and visible equivalent of that beautiful French chapel is right in my backyard. You walk down a small slope, along a narrow path, past a wall of pines, and suddenly you are standing in a vast cathedral of maples, even larger than the ancient chapel.

The glory part of my cathedral comes when the maple leaves are lit with purest sunshine, they glow red and gold against a ceiling painted with live sky-blue, and the forest floor is covered by an oriental carpet of new-fallen leaves and ferns, turned from green to autumn-gold. Great trunks, over eighty feet tall, and strong curved branches form gothic arches to hold up radiant crowns. You are in the quiet of a holy place.

I invite you to sit down among crisp leaves and to choose a comfortable tree to lean against. Wait . . . . Leaves take their time in their falling. Soon you will see an enchanting service: The Ballet of the Falling Leaves. As with snowflakes, no two leaves are alike. Some are half curled up, some flat, some yellow, brown, brilliant red or combinations of colors, some tiny, some large. Each descends in its own fashion. First you may see only one small leaf, alone in that vast space, flying free of its tree, then swinging off at an angle, and tucking into the carpet with a soft chuffy sound. Next, you may see two at once: in ballet language, a *pas de deux*. They swirl around each other, bowing, dipping, dancing. A small puff whispers to a tree and a whole chorus, corps de ballet, flutters down from it, spinning, somersaulting, skipping, some fast, some slow. A few get caught and decorate the shaggy bark of a hickory tree. You may notice one leaf doing a solo pirouette in midair, spinning so fast that it blurs; its stem has been trapped by an invisible spider web.

Moments pass when nothing falls, but don't be impatient. All at once, responding to a fair-sized breeze, a leaf-blizzard envelops you as hundreds of leaves drop at once, making that soft chuffy sound as they land. They drop right beside you, fall in your lap, kiss you on the head. Like Fourth-of-July skyrockets lighting up the whole sky during the grand finale, the whole forest is alight with gold and red flying leaves—up on the mountains, down the valleys, in and out among all the great trunks and branches. The forest is celebrating. REJOICE!

Night Happening

NOVEMBER NIGHTS in Vermont have magical qualities unknown to "leaf peepers" and summer visitors. Air is crisp, and bare trees make black lace across starry skies. On one such night, I decided to put a letter in the mailbox up by the road. I put on my hat, coat and mittens and called my dog, Josephine. We stepped out into blackness. With the help of a small flashlight for an occasional bearing, we reached the mailbox. By then I realized that the night was too beautiful to return to the house. All those stars! We started off for a walk down the hill.

We had not gone far when I heard a small rustling sound coming from the steep bank on one side of the road. I turned on the flashlight, expecting to see small bright eyes close to the ground. No eyes, just dead leaves and dried-up remains of wild flowers. We walked on. Then I heard it again, this time a bit louder and higher up. I admit to being scared. Suddenly I saw a huge black cow silhouetted against the starry sky. Then another and another, still more, all in a row and two sizes larger than in daylight, their Holstein white markings invisible. Only a strand or two of rusty barbed wire separated us. They were looking down at me from the top of the bank. We stood looking at each other in mutual amazement for several moments.

Then Josephine and I continued our walk. All at once I noticed that we were no longer alone. The whole herd of warm black bodies was walking with us down the hill on its side of the fence. For their size, they made very little noise—just a few snuffles and puffy sounds. When we turned around to go back up the hill, the cows came too. It warmed my heart, somehow. When we arrived back at the mailbox, the cows all lined up in a row, silent in the starlight.

Last Act

LATE FALL is the last act of a beloved opera. We know the plot but savor each final morsel before the curtain comes down and sends us out into the cold of winter. For two or three days after leaves have dropped, all the ground is pasted with gold leaf: acres and acres of that rare stuff. It shimmers on mountainsides, glows all along the banks of brooks and makes gold circles, like a child's crayon drawing of the sun, where maple leaves fall on green lawns.

I find it impossible to stay inside on these last days. I go off on my bike to the Rail-Trail and pedal slowly, lingering with the final fragments of autumn.

The whole tribe of woolly bear caterpillars is on the move. These wee prophets wiggle across the Trail and I try not to squash them under my tires. Where are they going? Why don't they stay on one side or the other? Chipmunks are in a panic. They dash around with bullet speed. "Have you been lazing around all summer like the grasshoppers?" I ask. No answer.

The sounds of late autumn are triste. Noisy harvesting machines are silent. Stripped cornfields testify to work well done. The aspen chorus is stilled. Canada geese have gone to Maryland cornfields, their high-up bell-barks no longer rouse answering barks from my small dog far below. Only a few crickets sing slow last love songs from browned grasses. A trio of drab birds in bare bushes utters subdued "cheep, cheeps." Bike tires crunch through dry leaves.

The low sun of late afternoon sets fire to the west slopes of hillsides and sends my shadow bumping over tired raspberry bushes, deceased goldenrod and exploding milkweed pods. Huge clouds cluster behind mountains waiting for the calendar to give them their cue to come rolling down into the valleys.

Intrepid, the weeping willow, ultimate prima donna, first to show green in spring, last to drop leaves in the fall, stands all alone in the lavender and gray scenery. Her long golden hair blows in the wind as the curtain drops. Farewell, autumn. Brava! Brava! Bravissima!

A Lonely Cricket and Others

WHEN THE CRICKET who lives in my computer room let out two loud chirps right after the dog barked, I was startled. I had become used to the cricket and am pleased to have him around. His chirp has a pleasant, resonant quality, bird-like, but definitely loud. At first he lived in my bedroom, but exactly where I could not discover. He throws his voice so cleverly that, though I looked, I could not locate him by sound. Recently he moved to the large ivy plant in the computer room. However, I have yet to see him. Why did this wee critter chirp at my dog Al? What is it with crickets?

Come to think of it, I have quite a few co-inhabitants in my house and, for the most part, we get along well together. In cities and suburbs, a distinct line is drawn between those who live inside and those who live outside. Not so in the country; there the line is sometimes fuzzy.

Because the fur coats on mice are so thin, mice have to move inside for the winter. They are not welcome. Traps snap. However, a few clever ones evade capture, resisting the temptations of baits of cheese or peanut butter. One such mouse lives somewhere in my kitchen, perhaps in the jungle under the refrigerator. It likes pears and it nibbles holes in them in the dark of night. It is alert and agile.

A bowl of nuts left just once on a counter was promptly invaded and the mouse had no trouble cracking the shells. How did it climb up the vertical slippery side of the cabinet without a rope or special shoes? No mountain climber could match its performance.

Mice are hoarders. Did you ever try to put on a boot and find it half full of sunflower seed? Once I found a cache of seeds under the bath mat in my bathroom: the result of many mouse journeys across the kitchen, across the living room, down a hall, past the sleeping dog and across my bedroom where I sleep.

And then there was the pound of choice pecans. One by one, without pausing to eat them, a mouse moved them from a lower pantry shelf to the far corner of a high shelf on the opposite side of the pantry. Like all survivors, mice work hard.

None of the various critters in my house has bitten me, neither spider nor wasp. They spend the winter on the plant bench and are not hostile. They move slowly among the leaves and probably help keep the aphids from chewing up the orchids. The recent invasion of ladybugs was a welcome addition. For a while I had a spider that wove a funnel web. Poor girl, what a boring life, waiting for something to fall into her trap. And then there was the wee caterpiller that spun a tiny cocoon on the rim of a sugar bowl . . . .

So, right here in my home, each critter goes about doing his or her own thing in his or her own way. Live and let live.

Winter

WINTER PICKS US UP and gives us a shake the way a mama dog shakes a misbehaving pup. She forces us to stop whatever it was that we were doing and pay attention. Have we been chasing too much trivia, attending too many meetings, running away from our own inadequacies? Winter is face-up time in Vermont. Winter attacks our vulnerabilities, knocks away grief, purifies us with tons and tons of sparkling snow.

Winter can be dangerous. Death hides in the huge icicles and avalanches that crash down from our roofs without warning. We understand the meaning of the windchill factor: winter clothes are serious clothes, and we know the importance of a wool hat, of layers, of keeping dry. We study the surfaces where we put our feet; a walk to the mailbox can end in broken bones so we take a ski pole to keep from slipping.

Winter sorts out friends from acquaintances. Friends phone to compare notes about the road, salted or not; power, on or off; water, frozen or not; furnace problems; and leaks and more leaks. Winter pokes her mean fingers into houses both young and old and finds all their multiple weaknesses. Intrepid plumbers, snow-plow drivers, telephone repairmen and fuel deliverers come to the rescue. Kindness and faithfulness beat back the cold.

The outdoor scene is full of complexities that change hour by hour and day by day. My birdbath acquires a three-foot-high dome. Only the antlers of the wooden reindeer on my lawn stick up out of the drifts. The woodshed has a new white roof made like a seven-layer cake, each storm adding another layer, with more to come.

Snowshoes are the way to go in the forest. Snow lifts us to a new level, high above ground. The extra height brings branches closer to our eyes and makes little brooks seem very far down. With an almost bird's-eye view, long-familiar trees look like strangers. Al tries valiantly to lead the way, making great leaps and sinking down to the tips of his ears, his whole face covered with snow. Soon he gives up and sticks close behind on my trail, now and then standing on the back of the snowshoes, bringing me to a sudden halt.

We grieve for the hungry deer, especially when ice has been added on top of snow. Animal tracks are few in deep snow. Small critters are down next to the ground where it is warmer and they can find seeds and roots to munch. They live in a snow-tunnel city of their own making. Like us, many forest critters put on warmer clothes: fur thickens, the squirrel's bushy tail curls up and keeps his back cozy, cardinals and blue jays fluff up their feathers (down jackets). Deer become invisible as their fur turns gray to match tree trunks. Weasels put on a glamorous white coat with a black tip at the end of their tail: ermine! Woodchucks, far under ground, snooze through the whole show. Winter.

Dirt Road People

DURING MY FIRST WINTER in Vermont, I found that a large part of my thinking was taken up with one subject: dirt roads. When I saw my friends, perforce sporadically, they greeted me in a manner which you would not hear in New Jersey—not "How are you?" or "What's new?" Rather their first question was, and still is, "How is your road?" I answer at great length, and they listen with compassion.

A bond ties together those of us who live on dirt roads. We talk with feeling about 180 degree spins on mud or ice. We discuss the route of the sander; some are lucky that school children live beyond their house because the school bus has priority with the sander. School comes first. We talk with feeling about deep ruts made by those heavy milk trucks . We know about driving along the edge of the road where sometimes it is not so slippery. I tell and re-tell about the time I skidded off my icy rainwater-glazed road and drove down Nate Smith's cornfield. The word "slippery" has a certain intensity for dirt road people.

We have a litany that goes like this:

Yes, I have four wheel drive.

No, it doesn't help on ice.

But that mud can get you too.

Yes, I would like to go to the dinner, the concert, the meeting . . . .

But I'm not sure I can get out.

Or, if I get out, if I can get back.

Frustration overwhelmed me for a while. When I was icebound, a mere half mile away the real world was still functioning, all oblivious to my desire to return that videotape eating up rental fees. I would pace the floor: to go down the hill or not to go down the hill, that was the question. I made it down one Christmas Eve with the help of those famous Christmas angels and a bag of kitty litter. That night I did a glissade, made the sharp turn at the bottom and crossed the bridge over the cold, black Mettawee River. I found that when a Jeep goes sideways down a hill it is very much like driving a refrigerator or a grand piano. Not funny.

Permit me to share my conclusions about all of the above: A pedant might say that one should be serious and recognize that the forces of nature in Vermont can be humbling. A drab conclusion. I don't look at it that way. For me it goes like this:

I check the big boulder at the end of my driveway. If it is covered with ice and the road is not sanded, I call up and cancel my obligations and preplanned delights with friends. Then I declare a holiday to celebrate the obvious fact that I have received a gift of freedom; a joyful day, like a snow day when I was in grade school; a holiday with no associated duties, no cards to send, no gifts to buy. I can re-read a favorite book, write a hot letter to the New York Times they will never print, make cookies, or even better, fill the house with the aroma of baking bread and, when it is done, eat big chunks of it with butter while it is still warm. I'm just a bit sorry when that intrepid sander shows up.

Napoleon the Squirrel

EARLY WINTER MORNINGS, I take a recycled plastic ice cream container and scoop up about a quart of sunflower seed from the supply in a large metal garbagecan on the porch. I pick my way over a bumpy, icy, and snowy path to the railing of the deck. The railing is comfortably wide for birds and other critters, and I cover about fifteen feet of it with seed. Then I pause, take a deep breath, look up at the sky-of-the-day with wonder, and say hello to God. By the time I am back inside, the whole railing is covered with birds.

The squirrels arrive a little later, but there is still plenty of seed left. I have two kinds of squirrels, red and gray. The gray squirrels are looking big, fat and prosperous these days. Their huge bushy tails, all fluffed out, curl over their backs and keep them cozy and warm. The red squirrels, half the size of grays, are doing all right too, but they rush around so fast they just don't have time to get fat.

One of the reds I have named "Napoleon." He is pure dynamite. He's probably the one who chewed the hole in the porch door and ate seed right out of the paper sack, whereupon I replaced it with the above-mentioned garbagecan. When he arrives on the scene, he clears it of all the birds, including Harry the hairy woodpecker and the gang of seven blue jays, those notorious bad guys of bird-dom.

For those of us with fragile egos who denigrate animals as unthinking instinct-driven creatures, what I now relate may come as a shock. One day, Napoleon had cleared off all the birds and was munching his way in a westerly direction along the railing. At the other end of the railing, a chubby gray was munching his way east. Slowly, they came closer and closer, both concentrating on breakfast. I wondered what would happen when they met.

Without missing a beat or a seed, Nappy looked up, saw the gray, made his plan and resumed eating. When they were about four inches apart, Nappy suddenly reared up on his hind legs to his full height. He struck like lightning. POW! With both front paws, he hit the unsuspecting gray with a mighty blow right to the chest. In a second, he had the whole railing to himself.

So there!

Window on Winter

EVERYONE LOVES those small glass balls filled with fake snow-flakes with their mini-scenes of pine trees, Santa Claus on a sleigh, or a tiny white church. Who can resist picking one up in a store, giving it a shake, then putting it down? For a brief moment you recapture the magic of a snowstorm. In a real Vermont snowstorm, the positions are reversed. We become the miniatures inside the glass ball, looking out at an enormity of a storm that has the power to bring the whole state to a halt.

In a blizzard I am drawn to the window, enchanted, half asleep and half awake. Falling snow hypnotizes like the flames of a log fire. Flames vary in direction as they dance their way to the chimney. Like snowflakes, no two flames are exactly the same color, shape and size. A hurricane has the same fascination. People defy the danger of wind and stinging sand to watch huge ungovernable waves roll in and crash on the beach, no two waves alike.

Snowflakes fall down but with variations. Some go off to the left, others to the right, some faster, some slower. A gust of wind can twist them into great spinning spirals that blow them off sideways to come to earth in the next meadow. As flakes gather on pines, their combined weight causes branches to suddenly bow down, creating a small snow waterfall that floats away like a cloud caught among the dark green pines.

Hungry blue jays, juncos and goldfinch gather for sunflower seed on my railing in front of the windows. Mourning doves puff up their feathers to keep their toes warm. Chickadees flutter close to me and make comments when I venture out to replenish their supplies. Harry and Harriet, my two hairy woodpeckers, arrive late. First they land on a vertical two-by-four that supports the railing. Then they climb it, and when they get to the top, they poke their rapier beaks high in the air and look all around. Only then do they attack the suet. Cardinals in snow are a beautiful cliché.

To watch a snowstorm is to turn off. Nothing else matters. Nothing can compete with the beauty of a living landscape. We let go all the doings that we thought we had to do, or might do, or would have liked to do. Friends, parties, rehearsals, meetings and concerts are all put on standby. Time goes as the sand in an hourglass while tiny flakes of infinite number pile up and engulf our lives, covering all our rough places with soft white pillows.

To watch a snowstorm is to see silence, winter's gift to a world abused by noise. No invisible symphony orchestra plays as in "nature" videos, with music synchronized to the flapping of flamingo wings. Silence is a physical necessity like the thirst of a dog after a long run. The psalmist said, "Be still and know that I am God." How is it that silence has become a luxury?

Winter is a vast and humbling presence. Winter defines Vermont more than red barns, black and white cows, and cheddar cheese.

Blue Gate

MANY YEARS AGO, my folks had a small cottage on the very edge of the waters of Barnegat Bay, New Jersey. The cottage had once been a boathouse. Alongside it was a tiny brick patio and, at its entrance, a small old wrought-iron gate with two latticed doors held together with many layers of sky-blue paint; each door had a scroll on top. The gate was always left open. You could see the bay just beyond it.

Friday nights, after a long ride from the north and a week of being seriously deskbound and responsible, the first thing I used to see as I drove into my folks' driveway was the blue gate and the bay beyond: my gateway to freedom.

I grew up on the bay, learned its sand bars, channels, winds, fog, places to drop anchor for lunch, gulls and shore birds, blue fish and blowfish, crabs. Best of all was the thrill of sailing when my boat came alive and lifted up with the wind as the main sheet was pulled in. I'm flying!

On water there are no sidewalks, traffic lights, speed limits, or asphalt parking lots. On water, elementary freedom to move where your spirit leads still can be found in this crowded world.

The old blue gate crumbled. My folks died. I sold the cottage.

Finally, I sold my sailboat, and with the proceeds, bought 40 acres of forest in West Pawlet, Vermont.

It took me a long time to figure out the similarities of forest and water. Forest has all the beautiful freedom of water. You can stay on a trail or wander off in any direction and not get lost, provided you are observant and watch the markers. No parking meters. So much to hear: the sounds of wind in treetops like the sound of waves breaking, the singing of birds at dusk, crickets. As on a sailboat, in the forest no two days are alike, early morning sunlight spotlighting the tree trunks, a spring flower, a sudden mushroom, or the leap of a deer. And great places where you can drop anchor for lunch. Like the watery world I used to inhabit, the forest is alive.

My land in Vermont is practically all uphill or downhill, depending on which way you are going. It has a large field of wildflowers, and a small level twenty-minute lawn with a tame-flower garden. The rest is forest. My garden needed a gate to the forest, to freedom.

Where could I find a gate? Back in Pine Beach, New Jersey where I used to live, I had two great neighbors: Ginnie who takes in old stray dogs and cats and her husband, Walter, a retired school teacher. Walter has a miniature iron foundry in his back yard, a shed about eight feet square with a dinky chimney. I mailed him a sketch of the old blue gate, told him to add anything to the design he wished and to paint it sky-blue. Months later he and a friend of his arrived in a truck with the gate. Ginnie had to stay home with the dogs and cats. The gate was already attached to stout wooden posts and painted the exact color I remembered. Of all the millions of shades of blue, he got it just right.

We had a gate-setting happening. Friends dug two deep holes using a crowbar to battle boulders. We took pictures, then stood around the gate in awe, touching it gently, swinging the hinges, trying the latch. More beautiful than the original, of incredible workmanship, made by a man who never had made a gate before but who likes poetry. It is both precise and charming. He added two small flowers set in ovals at the base, making the gate slightly taller than the original one. The scrolls at the top and the lattice below are perfect, a challenge to ironmongery, yet made in that tiny shop.

Now the blue gate stands, with both doors open where lawn and field touch. A short, rough path leads to the forest.

One winter we had a snowstorm that tapered off into an ice storm, coating every snowy twig, bowing down the pines, bending birches, coating the mailbox. The sky was strangely white, so that earth and sky became one, in matching silvered white. The blue gate stood out all alone in its color, shining in its transparent coat, floating, not earthbound in the all-white world.

I like to think that the gates of heaven are small and friendly, that they are painted blue, that they stand open to all, and that beyond them in heaven there are no sidewalks, maybe just deer trails.

Winter on the Rail Trail

DRESSED IN THREE LAYERS of clothes, with sheepskin mittens, a red wool hat, and Al to give me courage, I took off on Nordic skis to see what my favorite part of the Rail-Trail looked like in winter. I hadn't been on skis for at least two years and Al had never been out with me when I went skiing, this being his first Vermont winter.

We started in the center of West Pawlet at the bridge over the Indian River. Deep snow covered the floor of the bridge; snowmobiles had broken a trail. Al, intrepid, led the way. The river below was inky black, singing ice-music. All the boulders along the edge had vanished under puffy white blankets.

Beyond the bridge, the Trail cuts along the back of the village where in summer you can see well-tended gardens. Now only the tops of garden lanterns remained visible. The red brick walls of the old buildings of the village glowed in the brilliant winter light.

It was cold and dark in the part of the Trail that goes through the forest. The trail was icy, my skiing uncertain. I was glad when we came out into the sunlit valley, God's country. All that sky! We need to see it, especially in winter when we are often house-bound and nights are long. We need to look up at clouds, at hawks flying, at the long high contrails of speeding airplanes. And, oh, the joy of all that vast volume of crisp air, better than champagne: unrecycled air from the land of polar bears and penguins!

My ski-stride returns and soon I am warm and happy and so is Al, head up, eyes shining. He zigzags along about thirty feet ahead of me, investigating the edges, glancing back now and then. Suddenly, he plunges head first, half disappearing into the snow, chasing a critter. I catch up with him and wait. He is tireless, made for the outdoors.

I am moving within a live etching, unlike a watercolor or an oil painting of summer. Bare trees make dark patterns and arrange themselves against snow with all the complexity of a medieval tapestry. In winter, the artist's palette is different: every shade of blue, every tone of deepest darkest blacks and pearly grays, with lavenders and deep purple. In the sky, pinks and subtle greens with pale yellow at the horizon. To this, add an extravagance of sunlight on acres and acres of glittering snow.

Only the valley and the contours of distant hills remain to remind me of summer. In Vermont we live in two worlds.

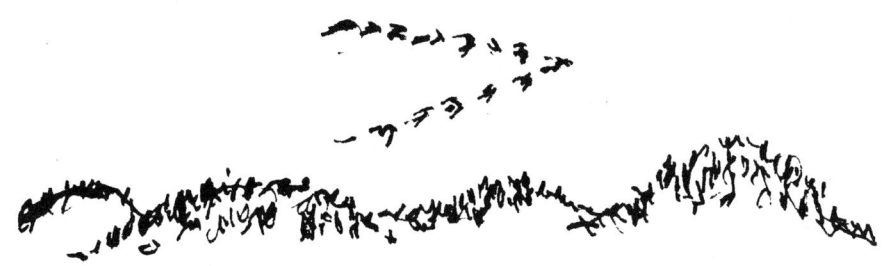

Tree Fall

AS SOON AS POSSIBLE after a big storm is over, I go into the forest with Al to check things out and to see if certain old favorite trees are still standing. Recently, after one such storm, we soon came upon a tall white pine, fallen.

It was stretched out, horizontal, in full rigging, like the great spar of one of those tall ships that sail into Boston Harbor now and then. Dead branches projected out from most of the trunk; live needle-covered branches were close to the top where they had found the sunlight. I stood beside the topmost branch of all and touched needles: gray-green, silky, so recently kindred to sky. I mourned that tree, beautiful, fallen. It had lived with clouds and stars, with swirling fogs, danced with winds and bowed to blizzards. It made a roost for a crow family that had a nest three trees away. It fed the small savage red squirrels with its cones.

As I touched that top, I realized I had entered into an otherwise inaccessible part of our world, like touching the outside of the top of the Empire State Building. I just stood there.

After a while I decided to measure the tree. I counted steps as Al and I walked its length about sixty feet to its huge clump of tattered roots. Raw numbers make for poor descriptions. Someone told me they measure by using imaginary six-foot-tall men. This tree would have needed a whole team of such men, standing on each other's shoulders. I wouldn't have liked to be the fellow on top.

While the Empire State Building is a whole lot taller, it was man-made, assembled. The amazing thing about the tree compared to that building was that the tree just grew, with no help from anybody at all, and starting from a tiny object considerably smaller than our littlest toe. It is to wonder.

We go about our daily business feeling big and important; we have things we must do: groceries to buy, letters to answer, people to call up. I suspect that we forget how small we are, really small. Al's legs are about eight or nine inches short and his chest clears the ground by less than four inches. But he doesn't know he is so short and I haven't told him, not that it would do any good if I did. In spite of his size, Al is a mighty self-important dog. He considers that he must keep the airplanes out of his sky, birds off his deck and trucks off his road. If he were much bigger he might be called obnoxious. His self-importance is laughable, especially so because he goes about his work with such gusto. But as we both stood beside that clump of tattered roots, it was very obvious to me that, compared to the tree, we were very close to being pretty nearly the same size.

A lot can be learned from a fallen tree.

A Christmas Gift

ON THE BEAUTIFUL DAY of the first snow, Josephine got bored with looking out the window while I worked on Christmas projects.

"Oh, come on, let's go out," she said while chewing on my shoe to get me going.

"Since you insist, let's go," I replied.

So I shut the door on all my chores and we stepped outside. It wasn't even cold. All was white. All was silent. My mind stopped its racing in and out the tangled web of lists and scheduled duties. Stillness floated down on snowflakes.

We set off down the small path that leads to the pine grove. Snow filtered through the pines but the thick layer of needles still showed brown under foot. Then Josephine led me on down to the shaggy remains of the old apple orchard.

We were in a white lace jungle. Raspberry bushes, wild grape vines, honeysuckle and other unidentifiable oddments were all blended into a white, soft unity. I stood still and let my eye wander in and out the network of snow-covered fallen branches, twisted trunks of old apples trees, rotting stumps, new saplings. Josephine made crunchy noises in crisp leaves hidden under the snow as she sniffed for rabbits. A chickadee rasped at us briefly. When I ducked under an old cedar, its branches bowed low with snow, a grouse shook me up with one of those noisy escapes that jangles the nerves of hunters.

As we worked our way back home again, I was thinking about how very different the forest was, with its white covering, from the way it had been just the day before. The gnarled twisted branches of untrimmed apple trees were as gnarled and twisted as ever, but in one brief day they had been transformed from being old and broken into an intricate work of art. All that we have done to our land, to scar it, to neglect it, to change it, to impose our wishes on it, all was blurred or obliterated. Original beauty was restored.

As we slowly walked back through the pine grove and up the path, it came to me that snow is like forgiving. When you forgive someone, or they forgive you, a personal world is transformed. Old injuries, while still there, just don't hurt any more. A miracle happens, a miracle still available from remote antiquity. Love returns, replacing anger.

I still don't know how to go about forgiving. I guess you just do it; the way a sportscrazy intrepid Frenchman in one of those hang gliders leaps off an Alp and soars over vast green valleys.

So forgive someone for Christmas and have a merry one.

Two Worlds

ONE VERY WINDY MORNING, close to New Year's Day, Josephine and I went into the forest; she to sniff about, I to see if I could clear off a certain trail that I share with the deer. I have known this trail ever since I started exploring my forest. It is a main trail going up the hill. Recent winds turned it into a shambles. Many of the ancient apple trees, once an orchard, had finally succumbed to the pines in their battle for sunlight. Twisted heavy black branches made giant tangles on the ground and trail.

To my considerable surprise, I found that the deer had taken charge of the whole matter. They had moved the trail twenty feet to the east. All I had to do for my own comfort was to break away a few high branches that can poke out the eyes of the unwary.

I circled back toward home and, as usual, paused at a favorite spot on a rocky ledge next to a clump of birch and hemlock trees. The ledge overlooks a miniature valley with a tiny spring-fed brooklet. The ground is squishy.

When I first visited this spot, the valley was filled with a giant game of jack-straws. Tall fallen aspens, birch and ash crisscrossed it so that it was impassable. In the few swiftly-passed years of my observation of this area, with no help from me, the forest floor was almost entirely cleared off: nature's silent recycling.

I reached out my right hand and grasped the small white birch beside me. I felt it quiver. Where had I felt that identical quiver before? My mind raced for an answer. It was a sailboat mast. I was anchored in a cove on my sailboat "Justice," sheltered from a storm on the Chesapeake.

The wind was ripping across the tops of my trees with the identical sound it makes in a small cove of the Tred Avon River. I was startled to see that the valley floor of brown leaves was overlaid with a thin veil of dancing blue water. I was standing in two worlds at once, my past and my present, a double exposure. I held the little birch for quite a while, then let go. Instantly, the blue waves vanished and I was back in the forest.

Do you suppose the deer will remember their old trail?

Possum Persistence

AT ABOUT THREE O'CLOCK one winter afternoon, I saw a baby possum* climb up the recycled Christmas tree on the deck outside my living room window. From there, the little guy easily reached the railing of the deck where I sprinkle sunflower seed and where I have a strong metal cage for suet. On that day, the cage happened to be filled with long strips of pork fat given to me by the friendly butcher at the Grand Union. He was all out of suet.

Heretofore, my encounters with possums had been limited to quick glimpses in headlights at night or squashed bodies on roads by day. This time I liked what I saw. My possum had a nice warm coat, white and fluffy underneath, with long gray guardhairs. Each tiny black ear was decorated with a flashy pink dot on top. Legs were covered with short black fur, well set off by shocking-pink hands and feet, each equipped with four fingers, a thumb and needle-sharp claws. His multi-purpose tail was long, black with a pink tip.

*I know it's supposed to be spelled "opossum." Never mind.

94

A pink button nose protruded from the end of a pointy, whiskery snout. By the way, possums don't make good pets. They have fifty sharp renewable teeth and can bite like bears, tigers and people.

The overall aspect of the small beastie on my deck was much more than the sum of his parts. His shape was that of a miniature submarine, tapered front and back and slightly bulged in the middle. On smoothly powered short black legs he stalked up to the suet cage with the deliberate slinky motion of a panther.

Two siblings followed him up the Christmas tree and to the railing. The smallest of the three was promptly bounced to the deck by the first arrival. The other sat down next to the cage, waiting for a turn, but soon gave up. Possums don't share.

Well, that number-one possum really tried. He attacked the cage with everything he had. He braced his body with his two hind legs, climbed on top of it, hung upside down and stretched every possible muscle and tendon. He seemed to be made of rubber. He lay on his stomach and hung on with one foot; he wrapped himself around every inch of that cage. He gnawed and he gnawed. From time to time, he stopped, sat up on his haunches and washed his face with his two front paws, like a cat. Then he went back at it, gnaw- ing some more.

I sat by the window, watching and trying to sketch the fuzzy writhings. Time passed.

I turned away for a few moments but almost immediately returned to the window. I had to know. Would he get it?

After about two hours, as it started to get dark and really cold, that little possum finally extracted a long strip of pork fat. I cheered. "You did it! You did it!" He didn't hear me through the double-paned glass. He retreated to the corner of the railing where he sat and ate the whole thing. There he stayed, full, dozing, nose resting on his front paws.

Once the coast was clear, one little brother possum returned, nibbled a few seeds on the deck, went up the Christmas tree to the railing and gnawed on the cage for a few moments and then quit. His heart was not in it. The other little brother never came back at all.

How little we know about those who share our world! One thing is sure: given equal equipment, the one with heart and persistence wins the fat that this world offers.

The Drums of Thaw

AH, BUT A FOREST is full of mystery! Just when I think I have explored it all, it tells me something more.

At the height of a recent thaw, I went into the forest to see what was happening to my two brooks. I could hear First Brook from my deck, so I knew she was up to something. She is a gentle brook whose waters slip out silently from a spring at the base of a rocky escarpment next to a white birch and a hemlock. She is narrow enough to jump over if your legs are long enough. She threads her way through the forest, gliding over boulders and making small waterfalls where fallen trees try to block her way. In winter, most of her surface is hidden under a thin coat of ice interspersed with holes through which you can see dark ripples and hear her talking to herself. Now, rushing flood waters from melting snow had shattered her icy overcoat and she was dancing, singing out loud, and throwing splashes into the air. Lovely, but I had seen this before.

Second Brook is farther into the forest. He comes tumbling down Oak Mountain, squeezes himself through a big pipe under the road, shoots out the other side and rushes on into my forest. He is not faithful like First Brook; he only appears for special occasions like spring and January thaws. What he lacks in constancy he well makes up for in splash; and I have just the place for him, a long deep gorge with pine-needle-covered sides and a clutter of jagged boulders at the bottom.

I stood watching from the edge of the gorge for a long time. It takes time to see such a sight: a feast of waterfalls; all the waterfalls anyone could ever want to see, too beautiful to count, the motion of water around ice-covered rocks, the pattern of the swirls, water splashing at the roots of an ancient birch . . . . And the sound of it.

After a while, I heard the drum.

When a symphony orchestra is playing full tilt, especially toward the end of a piece by Brahms or Beethoven, you are hearing many layers of sounds all at once, soprano flutes and violins, warm cellos, aggressive brasses, acid oboes. Kettle drums are the bottom layer, deep, resonant, a sound that blends in with all the other sounds but throbs: the beat of the giant heart.

The gorge cascade had just such layers of sound, soprano in shallow places, alto in deeper places, and blasts where water hit jagged boulders. A steady low booming came where the most water was falling from highest up and splashing into the deepest pools. A primitive sound. Long ago, cave-men must have heard it too. I could imagine them standing beside me, in all their shagginess, listening, rejoicing. I felt as one with them, glad that the long cold winter was over.

No wonder people love drums.

Still Life

I WOKE UP LATE one February morning, groggy and in a foul mood, shuffled in slippers and robe out to the garage attached to my house, and picked up my breakfast orange from a big bag on the floor. The garage is just the right temperature to keep fruit cool but not cold. On the way back to the kitchen, acting on some impulse that came from out of nowhere, I tossed the orange up in the air and caught it in one hand. The action startled me. How did I come to do that? I looked at the orange as if I had never seen one before.

The orange was unusually big. Its roundness fit my palm comfortably, neither soft nor hard, cool, not cold. The texture of the skin slightly bumpy, but velvety at the same time. Its color defied February, suggested October.

As I usually did, I cut it in thin slices from pole to pole so that the slices were half-moon shaped. But this day, I noticed the pattern of the slim cells full of juice and the transparent shiny covering that separated each cell. I cut each slice in half again, giving me a pile of bite-sized pieces that fit easily into the mouth without getting the fingers sticky. I took down the old dessert plate that I use all the time. On this day, I saw it anew as I looked at the orange. It is white with a wide turquoise-blue border that can only be described as ruffled with ridges touched with gold.

I put the orange slices on that old plate and was amazed. I was looking at a still life worthy of a Dutch artist: the blue, the flaming orange, the satin shine of the cells, the gold. I took it to the window seat where I usually read my way through breakfast. But not this day. Slowly, savoring the flavor, I ate that sweet, juicy orange, occasionally holding up a piece to admire its intricate structure.

When I had eaten it all up, I looked at the plate and peels: another still life! This one with a complicated design indeed: orange peels bright on the outside, cream colored on the inside, arranged all helter-skelter, and set off by the blue border of the plate; an even more difficult challenge for an artist. Each peel, now empty, was curled up like a wee boat with a pointy bow and a wide stern where a tiny elf might stand with an oar. Then I changed my mind. They weren't boats at all. Instead, I was looking at a plate full of curly smiles.

Potato Power

FEBRUARY IS A MONTH for withdrawal, for reading old books, for studying languages, for gazing out of windows, for cleaning the refrigerator. While I was engaged in the latter activity, I made a discovery.

The usual refrigerator is designed to hide at least a third of the contents way in the back, out of view and comfortable reach. The need to crouch on the floor to reach the back makes one reluctant to attack a refrigerator. The result is that long-forgotten odds and ends come to light only when a serious cleanup is undertaken.

On the bottom shelf, I discovered a potato, not particularly fat, about three by two inches. Either because of, or in spite of, its remote location, it had put forth several fair-sized shoots. It was really trying. I couldn't bring myself to toss it out into the February cold. So I put it in a small flower pot, covered it with earth, gave it a drink and tucked it between a rose-geranium and an orchid in the small greenhouse in my living room.

Its pale shoots promptly turned bright green. I watered it along with the rest of my plants but didn't pay any special attention to it. Not for long . . . .

That potato really grew. And grew. AND GREW! The shoots

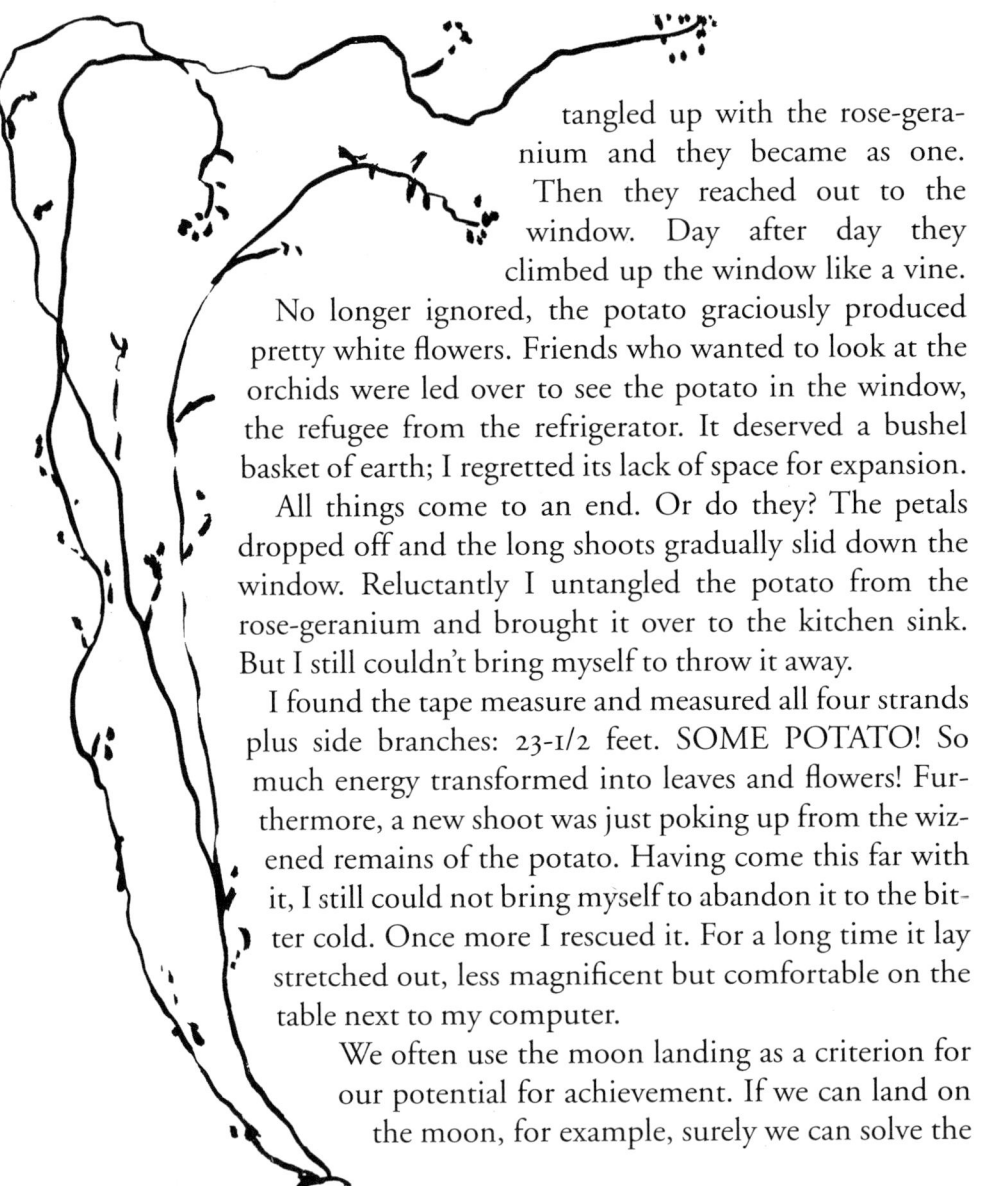

tangled up with the rose-geranium and they became as one.
Then they reached out to the
window. Day after day they
climbed up the window like a vine.
No longer ignored, the potato graciously produced
pretty white flowers. Friends who wanted to look at the
orchids were led over to see the potato in the window,
the refugee from the refrigerator. It deserved a bushel
basket of earth; I regretted its lack of space for expansion.

All things come to an end. Or do they? The petals
dropped off and the long shoots gradually slid down the
window. Reluctantly I untangled the potato from the
rose-geranium and brought it over to the kitchen sink.
But I still couldn't bring myself to throw it away.

I found the tape measure and measured all four strands
plus side branches: 23-1/2 feet. SOME POTATO! So
much energy transformed into leaves and flowers! Fur-
thermore, a new shoot was just poking up from the wiz-
ened remains of the potato. Having come this far with
it, I still could not bring myself to abandon it to the bit-
ter cold. Once more I rescued it. For a long time it lay
stretched out, less magnificent but comfortable on the
table next to my computer.

We often use the moon landing as a criterion for
our potential for achievement. If we can land on
the moon, for example, surely we can solve the

problem of making a toaster that doesn't burn the toast. I here suggest a better criterion for achievement. If one mediocre potato has the power and know-how to produce 23-1/2 feet of very attractive green stuff and decorate it with pretty white flowers, then why can't we, with all our fingers, toes, ears, eyes and alleged brains, do great things? Are we not as capable as a potato, oh ye of little faith?

Jewels of Winter

THE TRANSITION from winter to spring takes its own sweet time in Vermont. We put away our mittens only to bring them out again. Though skis are in the shed, the giddy yellow daffodils are flattened by snow. The chipmunk who scoots around my deck must use his wedge-shaped nose as a mini-snowplow to find sunflower seed.

Before winter finally dissolves into waterfalls and memories, I here report one last winter story from West Pawlet.

It starts with my grandfather, a jeweler for Tiffany's in New York. He used to bring diamonds home in his pocket to work on. He made all his own tools. He could engrave in complicated scrolls like the feathery frost designs on our winter windows. He was gentle, and he loved me. Perhaps by inheritance, perhaps by association, I have always admired meticulous artwork and beautiful stones. A thief stole my jewelry when I lived in New Jersey. Now I just look in jewelry store windows but do not go inside.

This winter, on one of those rare sunny days, I sat on my window seat eating lunch. I looked out the window and was amazed to see a real, live ruby blinking at me from a huge icicle hanging from the roof. It looked to be about three carats, clear, faceted and polished with all the brilliance and glow of the ones I once priced in Tiffany's.

"Just ice," you say. Well, yes and no. If you owned a stone ruby that big, you couldn't do any more than just look at it. You would be hit on the head if you wore it in public. It would lie dead in a bank vault most of the time, unseen.

My ruby, however ephemeral, was very much in plain sight and set in shimmering crystal. I marveled that such beauty could come from such simple ingredients: oxygen, hydrogen and sunlight. It takes twelve ingredients to make a carrot cake, not counting the icing, plus all the equipment. God certainly can do a lot with almost nothing—awesome.

I glanced down to take a bite of sandwich and looked out again. The ruby was gone. It had been transformed into an emerald, just as big and bright, a live vivid green. There it was, hanging right outside my window. Pure magic. Rubies are nice, but I always wanted an emerald. This jewel no one can ever take from me.

. . . And Three Dogs

Josephine

IT WAS THE DAY AFTER Labor Day and I was driving from Phila-
delphia to Toms River, New Jersey along Route 70, a monotonous
road that cuts through the Pine Barrens. It suddenly occurred to me
that I should hurry to get to the animal shelter in Forked River. I had
a very strong feeling that there was a dog waiting for me and if I
didn't hurry it would be gone. My little sheltie, Tiger, had died a few
weeks previously and my house was dogless; from childhood we had
always had dogs. I was bereft without one.

The animal shelter is huge, with two long wings divided into
metal cages on each side of the aisles. The place was jammed with
dogs as a direct result of the end-of-season brutality of summer visitors who drop off dogs along the highways as they return to the city.
Every possible breed and mixture of breeds was represented that day
from gorgeous Irish setters, blue-eyed Siberian huskies to the
plainest of mongrels. Two, three and four dogs were in each cage,
according to size; except for one cage.

As I walked down the aisle, all the dogs knew that I might be their
rescuer and take them home. They wagged tails, rubbed faces against
the heavy wire, looked directly in my eyes, pleading. One dog was in

a cage by herself, for everyone instinctively knew that there was something special about her.

She was shaggy all over, face, paws, ears, and long tail; whitish beige with a tinge of apricot; medium size. Her dark brown eyes were barely visible through the shag. I thought she was a mongrel but was told long after by a dog expert that she was a bearded collie, also known as a Scotch sheep dog.

She sat in the middle of the cage and lifted up one shaggy paw to me and silently but clearly said, "Help."

I will never forget my ride home with her, that great fuzzy nose next to my face. The next day I took her to show to a friend who asked me her name. Without even a moment's pause, to my considerable surprise, I said, "Josephine."

Until Josephine came to Vermont she had to live on the end of a leash. Vermont was her Paradise. She loved frisbees, skidding after them on pine needles, just missing tree trunks. She happily demolished frisbee after frisbee. I still find bits of colored plastic in the forest. It was beautiful to see her flow through a field. If the grass was over her head, she would leap straight up in the air to get a glimpse of the terrain.

She delighted in wild turkeys. On one joyful day, she almost caught one by the tail as it struggled to become airborne. One evening a large flock roosted way up in the top of the tallest pines near the cabin. Far below, Josey woofed and woofed and finally blew the whole bunch away.

She taught me to find my way along deer trails and never let me get lost. Josephine always found the shortest way home. She was welcomed everywhere and waited patiently through meetings of the church ladies' guild and bell choir rehearsals, shedding white fur on red carpet.

Cross-country skiing with Josey had unique thrills. I would go zooming down one slope of my neighbor's hayfield while she bounded down another. We managed to miss each other at the bottom by inches. On a certain unforgettable day, when it was time to go home, I couldn't see her anywhere. I looked out over acres of empty whiteness and called and called.

I finally turned and looked behind me. There she was, waiting for me, sitting on the back of my skis.

We looked alike, as happens with dog owners. We both had shaggy white hair and brown eyes. You could tell us apart because she was the one with the black nose: Josephine.

Love Story

WHEN I BOUGHT AL, I soon found that I had joined a very special club. Corgi owners are instant friends, bonded even though their own dog may be long since dead. They jam on their brakes when they see someone with a Corgi walking down the street and they get out of the car to compare Corgi experiences. They go out in rain or snow to greet a Corgi waiting in a friend's parked car. When they meet on the street, their first question is: "How is your doggie," or, "How is Al?"

I grew up with dogs and bought an Irish setter with my very first pay check. But of all the many successor dogs in my life, I never had one remotely like Al. Corgies look like another one of God's many jokes; consider frogs, grasshoppers, turtles.

The funniest of many funny things about Al is his physical design. He is both big and small. His chest barely clears the ground because his legs are so short. In certain positions when he lies down, his legs completely disappear. His body is long and heavy. If he decides not to do something he can turn himself into a rock, thus leaving his tugging owner suddenly holding a leash with an empty collar. His rear end is rounded off because his tail is docked. Lack of tail does not inhibit his expression of joy, however, because he can wag his whole rear end.

Odd shape is redeemed by other features. He has beautiful thick fur in variegated shades of gold with snow-white chest and paws. Mud doesn't stick to it. He can smell a cookie at fifty yards. He loves to play. Best of all are his infinitely expressive, soul-searching, dark-brown eyes.

Corgi ears have the quality and almost the size of deers'. Al can hear through double glass windows when a mouse tiptoes across the grass outside. He wakes up from a sound sleep in the far end of the house when I break an egg in the kitchen. He can wiggle his ears alternately to attract attention. When he runs, he cuts down-wind resistance by flattening them close to his skull. He also flattens them down to express both joy and anger and gets them out of the way for pats. Al has no hangups about expressing emotions. See below . . .

"Al" is a nickname. His kennel name is "Allegro Vivace," a composer's designation on musical scores for a fast and lively tempo. Al has the pick-up of a Porsche and the reflexes of a star quarterback. He catches flies in midair. Corgies used to earn their living herding cattle. Al still knows how. He tried it on one of John Malcolm's cows once, and it worked. I have been told that Corgies used to take lunch to their masters working deep in Welsh mines. It is also said that this ancient breed pulled wagons for the fairies. They do resemble elves, somehow.

All of which brings me to the emotion factor.

Corgies are born manipulators. When I bought Al home, a six-week-old, five-inch-tall, fuzzy pup, he strutted around my living room with all the self confidence of General MacArthur. He knew who he was and was not shy about it. He expected me to come to him instead of the other way around. As a pup, he had needle-sharp teeth that he used with determination. It was him or me. I took him to Doreen, an experienced dog trainer in Rutland. She taught me how to crouch down, flip him on his back, stare into his eyes until he looked away, all the while holding his jaws and growling "NO BITE." It worked.

We have a truce. He has his job, I have mine. He takes pride in keeping airplanes from hanging around my sky and too many birds from cluttering up my trees. Raccoons, skunks and possums stay away, and squirrels get plenty of exercise. His ringing bark carries to the river. When we walk in the forest he always goes first, once he figures out where I am going. He peeks back frequently to be sure I'm with him. He knows I won't always follow, and he doesn't want to get left behind.

He is sociable. He likes to go visiting, and when I have a party he walks around the room and greets each person. If I go away for a few days and leave him in a kennel or with friends, he gets really mad and won't talk to me for a whole day. He has a variety of voices and has taught me what they mean. He bounces a ball at my feet to come play hide-and-seek or run-and-catch. He loves to be brushed, snuggles up like a big pussycat, and does everything but purr.

He warms my heart.

Drift

LATE ONE ICY NIGHT in February as I was sitting by the stove reading, I heard a sound at the door. I got up, turned on the porch light, and saw a large black dog sitting on my doormat. It was no night for a dog to be out, so I let him in. He was soaking wet, limping. At a word, he sat down by the stove, obviously a well-trained dog. He had a Pawlet dog tag but no other name tag so I would have to wait until morning to find his owner. I dried him with my biggest bath towel and pulled off several clusters of burdock stickers tangled in his thick, long fur. I put him to bed in the garage on an old rug with some of Josephine's dog food and a bowl of water.

The next morning I let him into the house. He was a changed dog, all smiles, tail wagging, a real charmer, no limp. Tall, the kind of dog you don't have to reach down to pat, white nose, white chest, brown spots over soulful brown eyes: a presence.

With the help of our town clerk Joanne Waite, I located his owners, Amy and Peter Helmetag. In no time, Peter was at my door, relieved to find their dog. The reunion of dog and master was deeply felt. Peter is well over six feet. By way of a special greeting the dog stood up on his hind legs, with his paws touching Peter's shoulders. Almost face to face, they both stood silently for several moments, looking into each other's eyes. They clearly understood each other. Peter told me that the dog's name was "Drift." He looks after Peter's sheep, but when his sheep-work is done for the day, he gets bored and sometimes manages to break loose and disappear. At a word from Peter, Drift jumped into the back of Peter's truck and off they went. Not the end of this story.

Months later, summer with the doors wide open: I was in the kitchen and all at once, without a sound, there was Drift, tail wagging, big happy smile, pink tongue hanging out, eyes shining. Josey came in, pleased. Drift slurped up Josey's water and I gave them both a dog biscuit, an impromptu dog party. They both ran out and romped around in the garden like three-year-olds at a birthday party.

"This won't do, I must take him home," I thought. So I opened the back of the station wagon, called the dogs who immediately jumped in, and off we went. As I looked at the two dogs in the rearview mirror they were a sight that sticks in my mind, a cherished memory, probably my only worthwhile rearview mirror memory. The two dogs were sitting up straight, still, and proper, like two of my church people taken out for a ride, happy, enjoying. Across the bridge over the Mettawee River, down the road to the highway, down the highway to Peter's and Amy's bridge, back across the Mettawee River and up their hill, past the sheep to their house, a total of about two miles. Neither dog moved a muscle the whole way. I left Drift off in the front hall as both owners were at work.

I never knew when Drift would come back again, but it was always a great surprise and a delight. One day as I was sitting at the computer, all of a sudden, without a sound, there he was, right at my shoulder, big smile and all. Another time he scared the daylights out of a friend staying at my house while I was away. She was sleeping on the living room sofa and suddenly there was this big black dog . . . . Whenever he came, it was dog biscuits all around, water slurped, game of tag in the garden and that very proper ride home. Our friendship lasted for years, outlived Josephine and continued with Al, a funny combination.

Never was a dog more aptly named than Drift. With his long legs and strength he could cover ground with incredible speed. He could make it to my house in less than five minutes. He also had a long-distance gait. I saw him trotting along the edge of a road one day. There was something about the way he put down his paws, the flow of his gait, like a wolf, primitive competence, effortless, designed to cover several counties. He was on his way with some definite goal in mind. I didn't stop him.

I am aware that he was a con-man par excellence, but I am sure I was not his only friend, and so I do not feel guilty about encouraging his roaming by giving him a dog biscuit once in a while.

Dogs and people die and it certainly hurts those left behind, but dogs and people live on in our memories. When I go down that road I can still see Drift on his way, a free spirit. Sometimes, like now, when I am typing, his big head is right at my left shoulder, his tongue hanging out, eyes shining. "How about a dog biscuit?"